ECCLESIASTES
The Life
without God

James T. Draper, Jr.

ECCLESIASTES

The Life without God

G. Allen Reece Library
Columbia International University
Columbia, SC 29203

Tyndale House
Publishers, Inc.
Wheaton, Illinois

Scripture references,
unless otherwise noted,
are taken by permission
from *The Living Bible*, © 1971,
Tyndale House Publishers, Inc.,
Wheaton, Illinois.
Other references are from
the King James Version (KJV).

Library of Congress
Catalog Card Number 80-53684
ISBN 0-8423-0681-1, paper
Copyright © 1981
by James T. Draper, Jr.
All rights reserved.
First printing, March 1981
Printed in the
United States of America

CONTENTS

1. Life without God *1:1-11*   7
2. The Foolishness of Wisdom *1:12-18*   15
3. Living for Pleasure *2:1-3*   23
4. The Work Ethic *2:4-8*   29
5. The Success Syndrome *2:9-11*   38
6. The Tyranny of Time *3:1-9*   46
7. Our Sovereign God *3:10-18*   51
8. The Inequities of Life *4:1-3*   59
9. Someone to Care *4:7-12*   67
10. Dangerous Worship *5:1-7*   75
11. The Peril of Wealth *5:10-17*   83
12. The Frivolous Spirit *7:1-6*   90
13. Obedience in Adversity *11:1-6*   98
14. Coming Judgment *11:9, 10*   106

Life without God
Ecclesiastes 1:1-11

"THE WORDS OF THE PREACHER, the son of David, king of Jerusalem. Vanity of vanities, saith the Preacher, vanity of vanities; all is vanity. What profit hath a man of all his labour which he taketh under the sun?" (1:1-3, KJV).

That sounds rather ominous—a very discouraging and depressing beginning for a book. To understand such a beginning, it is necessary to understand the position from which the writer of Ecclesiastes is speaking. Life without God is the theme of the book of Ecclesiastes. It is a picture of life lived in sheer human energy, in total human ingenuity. Therefore, in the book we are immediately faced with "vanity of vanities; all is vanity" (1:2, KJV).

We must understand that this book was written in hard times. The nation of Israel was in difficult straits. The people were pressed down. Oppression was common, and because of it, there was much discouragement and despair. People had come to value earthly things too highly and expected too much from their possessions. When their expectations weren't met, they became discouraged and disappointed. The writer of Ecclesiastes was trying to put the things of this world into proper perspective. His thesis was that if we learn what we can expect from this world, we will not expect too much and become depressed and disappointed.

The author called himself "the Preacher" (1:1). The

word in the Hebrew is *koheleth*. Many Bible commentators accept this as a proper name. *Koheleth* is the feminine form of a word which identified "one who addressed a multitude or an assembly of people." The writer of Ecclesiastes delivered this message as one in an official capacity.

It is as though he had brought all of the people together to explain to them the message that God had laid upon his heart. He was, indeed, the Preacher, whether *koheleth* be a proper name or whether it be understood as a designated title. He was nevertheless going to dispense some of God's wisdom and counsel. He was called "the son of David, king of Jerusalem." Most scholars believe that David's son, Solomon, wrote this book.

The theme that the author developed in the opening verses runs throughout the book. "Vanity of vanities, saith the Preacher, vanity of vanities; all is vanity. What profit hath a man of all his labour which he taketh under the sun?" (1:2, 3, KJV). Certain truths in these two verses will help us understand the message. The Hebrew word for "vanity" means "vapor" or "breath." It could be described by the vapor seen when we breathe in freezing weather. A mist appears, then, in a few seconds, it vanishes. That meaning of the word speaks of something transitory, fleeting.

To interpret the word only as something that is passing away would be to miss much of the meaning as used here in Ecclesiastes. For instance, it not only means something that is passing away, but something that is utterly hopeless, completely empty, and pointless. The word speaks of meaningless desperation. Everything is futile, passing by so quickly that there is no purpose in it at all.

Note also the little phrase, "under the sun," which is used twenty-five times in Ecclesiastes. The word "vanity" is used at least thirty-one times. Without the phrase, "under the sun," we have statements in Ecclesiastes that border on heresy. The Preacher was saying that if we view life simply as life "under the sun," simply as a temporal existence, we will find the vanity he described, the pointlessness, the transitory nature of the things of this life—the vain, futile things that are wrought by human energy.

He was building a case to show that everything we can produce in our own strength is futile. Our best logic, our best efforts to be good and moral are nothing but futility. There is no meaning or purpose to it. It is all done "under the sun." By speaking of the things that are done in human energy and by human flesh, the author was pointing us to something higher. Life does not have to be empty and pointless. We do not have to be victims of the transitory nature of time and life. We can live on a higher level than that. The theme he projected throughout the entire book is that all is vain if we live only in the power and energy of our flesh.

"What profit hath a man of all his labour which he taketh under the sun?" (1:3, KJV). Obviously we get something for all the energy we put into life. The author of Ecclesiastes was not saying that we cannot achieve some things in the energy of the flesh. When we work hard and do the best we can, we do get something for it. But, the author said, we don't get much, nor does it satisfy as we would have hoped. We don't get lasting satisfaction or joy. There is pleasure in sin "for a season," but not for long. The man who works and lives without any thought or awareness of God is living his life in vain. His life has no point or meaning, nor does he enjoy real success or lasting achievement. There is no purpose, meaning, or direction to his life, the Preacher said.

THE ILLUSTRATION
"One generation passeth away and another generation cometh: but the earth abideth for ever" (1:4, KJV). In the

Hebrew, the words describing one generation passing and another coming are participles. One generation is always passing off and another is always coming on the scene. It's an endless procession. This verse does not imply that the earth is eternal, nor that its matter is everlasting, but that the earth is the solid foundation upon which this drama is taking place. The earth remains, the people change.

It is frightening to consider that years ago people just like us, who had the same frustrations and the same problems, lived here. Modern ingenuity and technology may have created new problems, but only new in their expression—not new in their kind. People have always had the basic frustrations of childhood and growing up. They have always faced basic temptations to be immoral and dishonest. They have fought the basic problems of jealousy, envy, and pride. The people who lived before us have gone through the same things we are going through. A hundred years from now, if the world still stands, there will be another group of people having the same kinds of problems. In some ways we are simply a part of an endless rat race, a continuous changing of faces upon the stage. One generation is coming, another generation is moving out. It appears that the actors change, but the stage remains the same and the same meaningless drama continues.

In verses five through seven, the writer used the sun, wind, and rivers to further illustrate his thesis. All of these reveal a universal sameness, an unwearied procession of cycles. Life simply goes on. To those who live without God, there appears to be only a continual turning again of the same thing.

Someone said, "A dewdrop is just as beautiful as a diamond." Too bad there is no market for dewdrops. Whoever heard of a young man giving his fiancée a dewdrop just because it is as beautiful as a diamond? True, its beauty may be the same, but it has no permanence. The writer of Ecclesiastes is illustrating that without God, life has no lasting value. Without God we simply go through the cycles, the same motion of the sun rising and setting and rising again, the winds circling and turning and coming back again, the river flowing to the sea and coming back to its source again, generation after generation moving endlessly upon the stage of this life. Without God, that is how life appears to be.

Ecclesiastes is not the sad dissertation of a pessimist—someone complaining about how terrible and futile life is. Although he reminded the reader that life apart from God is futile, he also implied that inside all of us there is a desire to do more than just exist, to do more than just be a part of an endless procession of faces upon the stage of life. God has given that desire to us, but if we try to live without God, we will defeat the purpose of that desire. If we give our lives to God, we fulfill that desire and have a sense of purpose, direction, and permanence about our lives.

THE CONCLUSION

Notice the writer's conclusion: "Everything is unutterably weary and tiresome. No matter how much we see, we are never satisfied; no matter how much we hear, we are not content. History merely repeats itself. Nothing is truly new; it has all been done or said before. What can you point to that is new? How do you know it didn't exist long ages ago? We don't remember what happened in those former times, and in the future generations no one will remember what we have done back here" (1:8-11).

The Preacher said that life apart from God is wearisome. All things are hard. All things are oppressive, so much so that man cannot utter them. Words can't express the frustration that bears upon our souls from time to time. Many have come to a moment of complete despair and of wanting to explain it but cannot. Apart from God, life is such a riddle, an anomaly, a paradox, a contradiction that man cannot comprehend.

Apart from God, the Preacher said, our eyes will see things that will never bring satisfaction. Our ears will hear things that will never satisfy. That was the conclusion of the Preacher.

These verses do not mean that there have never been new inventions. But inventors never discover anything that wasn't already here.

Others have faced the problems we now see. Sometimes we feel that no one understands, that no one has ever been through what we are experiencing. But they have, thousands of times. There is nothing new under the sun. Or we may think that no one has ever known the power of God as we do. Yes, they have. It has all been done before. There is nothing new under the sun.

That could be a discouraging truth. But it can also be extremely exciting. We can look back into the past and see the moving of God in mighty acts of power and know that since it has been done there, it can be done again. The power of God that has been demonstrated in the lives of his people down through the years is still available to us today.

It is a tragedy that we do not seem to learn from the past. "We don't remember what happened in those former times" (1:11). We don't seem to remember what has happened before. There is a tremendous hunger, tremendous weariness, and tremendous frustration in doing much but getting little out of it.

A great deal of energy, activity, and intellectual knowledge is poured into things and we forget how very little we receive in return. The more money we make, the more we want to make. The more public acclaim we get, the more we want. There is no end in our search for satisfaction. Every experience seems to say, "Here is something else to get!" No matter how much we achieve, there always seems to be something more. The building of a home, the building of a business, the building of a community are all good things, but even in these there is emptiness.

The writer of Ecclesiastes exposed life's emptiness and created a hunger for something better—something fulfilling. Every message in Ecclesiastes ends the same way. The underlying message is that life does not have to be lived on the low level of human understanding. In God we find the answer to the frustration and emptiness of the world around us. There is a better way than the bitterness and strife that tears at the business community. There is more than the hatred and violence that gnaws at the very foundation of our society and at the relationships between nations. There is a better way, and that way is found through a discovery of God, who alone is eternal. He alone can change a dewdrop into a diamond and give permanence and meaning to life.

Christians need to be warned that even their activities can be described by the word "vanity." Many Christians work hard, do their best, but they measure their Christian experience by certain achievements. Often they are endeavoring to live the Christian life on a purely human basis, which cannot be done. There is something better than that. We must come to the place of utter hopelessness. The only way we can be the Christians we ought to be is for Jesus Christ to live his life through us. Jesus Christ must give purpose, meaning, and value to our lives.

The message of Ecclesiastes is directed to the person who is caught in the endless, frustrating, empty cycle of life. The Preacher declared that there is something better. That better thing is found in God through Jesus Christ.

*Life
without God*

For those of us who claim to know Christ as Savior and yet have found life bound in the same vicious cycle of monotony and emptiness, there is a better way. It is to surrender completely, to be obedient to him so that he can live his life through us—his eternal, unchanging life.

2 The Foolishness of Wisdom
Ecclesiastes 1:12-18

ONE WAY man tries to find happiness is through gaining earthly wisdom and knowledge. The Preacher began immediately to show how this pursuit also is folly and vanity. "I gave my heart to seek and search out by wisdom concerning all things that are under heaven" (1:13, KJV). The word "heart" in the Hebrew means the individual's mental faculties, so it can properly be interpreted "mind." "I have made up my mind; I have chosen to give myself to the pursuit of earthly wisdom."

Obviously the author was speaking of "worldly" wisdom. All of these rather startling conclusions seemed to have been drawn from the energy of human understanding. He was talking about life without God, about wisdom not founded upon God's mind and God's purpose. With no reference to God as his source, he wrote that he had magnified and increased in wisdom more than all who were over Jerusalem before him.

Wisdom was the instrument by which he would test all of these things. We understand earthly wisdom to mean the very best thinking a man can do, the very best intellectual pursuit, the very best logic. All this takes place, however, "under the sun," in the sphere of fallen man, where everything is tainted by sin. So for the sake of argument, the author showed what results from trying to solve

The Foolishness of Wisdom

the problems of mankind by the rational thinking of sinful man.

In this chapter, we are watching the man who says, "I have to figure it all out. I have to understand everything by logic. I must develop my mind and sharpen my wits in order to learn all that life means." Here is the pursuit of an explanation of the mysteries, fallacies, and injustices of life.

This is not a new pursuit, as others have done it before us. Some would have us believe that the way to solve all the world's problems is through sharpening the intellectual capacity of mankind. Even a brief view of history would reveal the fallacy of such reasoning.

HUNGER FOR KNOWLEDGE
Man has an insatiable hunger for knowledge. "The lot of man, which God has dealt to him, is not a happy one" (1:13). It is important to see that God gave man this hunger. Even though some people do not know God, all feel a deep urge to discover truth. Man has an inquisitive soul, a searching heart, an inquiring mind—because God made him that way. But the author made it clear that the pursuit of knowledge is a difficult, unrewarding task. The search for wisdom is not wrong in itself, but it is wrong for man to seek for wisdom outside of God. The frustration people face comes from seeking wisdom in the wrong place. They ask the right questions to the wrong people. They seek to determine truth with the wrong tools. God warned us in advance of the disappointment that would come because of our wrong expectations. The Preacher's search for wisdom did not produce the desired results. He told us what the conclusion was: that insatiable hunger for knowledge did not satisfy. Throughout all Ecclesiastes we see that there is no satisfaction outside of God.

Ecclesiastes 1:12-18

AN INABILITY TO CHANGE

Even if man could satisfy his hunger for knowledge, the writer of Ecclesiastes said that even this wisdom to explain life wouldn't give man the ability to change it. "That which is crooked cannot be made straight: and that which is wanting cannot be numbered" (1:15, KJV). As he wrote later, "Consider the work of God: for who can make that straight, which he hath made crooked? In the day of prosperity be joyful, but in the day of adversity consider: God also hath set the one over against the other, to the end that man should find nothing after him" (7:13, 14, KJV). The author was painting a picture of the inability of man to change life by the wisdom he seeks to discover. We cannot, by finite reasoning, change the circumstances of life. We cannot alter what is unjust. We cannot bring perfection out of imperfection by our finite minds. Man by himself cannot correct the ills and tragedies of this life. This world is a vale of tears. Everywhere there are discomforts, needs, wants, heartaches, troubles, and fears. Man by himself is unable to do anything about it.

Thus far, man in his search for wisdom finds himself confronted with inexplicable inequities, difficulties, and problems because he has left God out of his search. Most of us, when we have made up our minds, think we are the only ones who need to be consulted. Our political leaders meet, make up their minds, and declare what they will do without consulting the One who really has the say about what happens. They have left God out of their plans.

Earthly wisdom only reveals problems—it does not solve them. A comprehensive quest for wisdom soon leads us to understand that we are not achieving anything. We have a sense of restlessness because of the injustice and the despicable evil things in life. But we are reminded that God is still God and that both good and evil can be made to achieve his purposes, as the Preacher said: "Enjoy prosperity whenever you can, and when hard

The Foolishness of Wisdom

times strike, realize that God gives one as well as the other" (7:14). Paul the Apostle wrote years later: "All things work together for good" (Rom. 8:28, KJV). All things? Does all include bad things as well as good things? Of course it does! God is not bound by the mistakes of man. Nor is he bound by the attacks of Satan. Good and evil, prosperity and adversity, God uses it all.

Without God, life is an illogical, hopeless situation. When we look at the world through human reasoning, it appears to be nonsensical. But when we look at it from God's perspective, it all falls into place. God still uses adversity and prosperity, the good days and the bad days, to achieve his purposes. We are not to presume that God designs evil. The Apostle James makes it clear that God is not evil, that he does not tempt man to do evil, and he cannot be tempted with evil (James 1:13). There is enough evil in human nature and in the presence of Satan himself to create many, many acts of evil and many, many days of adversity, but God is not bound or crippled by any of them. He is still working through the world to achieve his purposes. But after we gain earthly wisdom, we discover that we cannot change life.

THE EMPTINESS OF EARTHLY WISDOM

The writer pointed out the emptiness of the world's wisdom. "So I worked hard to be wise instead of foolish—but now I realize that even this was like chasing wind. For the more wisdom, the more my grief; to increase knowledge only increases distress" (1:17, 18). When we seek earthly wisdom, we learn some discouraging things. We can enjoy our prosperity and luxurious living until our search for wisdom reveals that thousands of people starve to death from malnutrition each day and that most of the people of the world do not enjoy even the simple things we take for granted. In our quest for wisdom, we might experience a distress that will not let us enjoy what we once enjoyed. Knowledge can often bring distress and grief to our hearts.

Such wisdom brings the kind of pain the King James Version of the Bible calls grief and sorrow. It is the result of knowing something is wrong but not being able to do anything to stop it. We learn in the next chapter that death treats the wise man and the foolish man alike. Wise men die and so do fools. It seems so unfair. No matter how far up the ladder of intellectual pursuit we have climbed, we will die. More than that, we will be forgotten (2:16). We are not only going to die like the fool, our wisdom is going to be forgotten after we are gone. What an empty pursuit knowledge is—apart from God.

Earthly wisdom also causes us to develop a false righteousness. The Preacher spoke of a lifetime of futility in which a righteous man perishes in his righteousness (7:15, 16, KJV). He is talking about false righteousness, self-righteousness. When we begin to climb the ladder of intellectual success and achievement, we begin to develop a hypocritical pose and we belittle other people. Jesus talked about this attitude in the Sermon on the Mount when he said, "But I warn you—unless your goodness is greater than that of the Pharisees and other Jewish leaders, you can't get into the Kingdom of Heaven at all" (Matt. 5:20). The pursuit of earthly wisdom produces a hypocritical, self-righteous spirit.

The emptiness of wisdom also brings about a short-lived gratitude. Later on, the Preacher told the story of a city that was about to be attacked by the enemy. A very poor man, by his wisdom and ingenuity, delivered the city. He fooled the enemy and saved the city. But no man remembered that poor man (9:13-18). The pursuit of wisdom leads us to the emptiness of trusting in the public praise and gratitude of other people. Those people who praise us the most will be the first to criticize us. Earthly wisdom seeks to achieve a level of human approbation, of public praise. But it is empty. The same people who sang hosannahs to Jesus cried, "Crucify him," a few days later. It is an age-old story. Those who think that reaching certain intellectual plateaus of earthly wisdom is true achievement find instead that emptiness is only deepened.

THE ADVANTAGE OF EARTHLY WISDOM

There are some advantages to earthly wisdom. God wants us to be as wise as we possibly can. He wants us to develop our intellects. The tenth chapter of Ecclesiastes outlines some advantages for us. First, wisdom insures success. The author uses the illustration of a man chopping down a tree. If the man is smart, he will sharpen the axe. Otherwise, he will have to use more strength. That is simply using wisdom to one's practical advantage.

Wisdom not only insures success, it helps one foresee problems. The author used two illustrations for this point. The axe was one. If the dullness of the axe is foreseen, it will be sharpened. The other example was of a snake who bites before it has been charmed. There is no need to charm a snake that has already bitten. A wise man will charm the snake before getting close to it. That is wisdom. Earthly wisdom helps us foresee problems.

Third, wisdom helps us use words cleverly. The author told us to be wise in our choice of words. "The words of a wise man's mouth are gracious: but the lips of a fool will swallow up himself. The beginning of the words of his mouth is foolishness: and the end of his talk is mischievous madness" (10:12, 13). No one wants to be a fool or to be laughed at. We like for people to think we have it all together. Wisdom helps us to use words cleverly. But notice that underlying the clever use of words, the author

Ecclesiastes
1:12-18

pinpointed a subtle attitude. A man may be smart enough to use the right words, but refuse to begin with God. Many people know all the language of the church but they are not saved because they refuse to begin with God. Some of the most unbelievable sins are justified by people who claim to be saved. They know the right words to say about repentance, conversion, and salvation, but an underlying attitude belies the words they say. Wisdom helps us to use words that put us in a good light with other people. But our wisdom must begin with God.

Wisdom gives confidence. "A wise man is stronger than the mayors of ten big cities! And there is not a single man in all the earth who is always good and never sins" (7:19). Wisdom gives us confidence even in the face of opposition. Knowing the truth gives us an advantage even over the strong.

However, as we read the conclusion of these passages, we come back to the same result—vanity, futility, and chasing after the wind. The vanity of earthly wisdom needs to be driven into our hearts. Many of us will never come to God until we have emptied ourselves of earthly wisdom, until we have done everything our minds tell us to do, and see the emptiness of it. Many people are waiting until they understand everything about redemption before they give their hearts to God. It is the typical response of those depending on earthly wisdom, who are trying to figure everything out. Whole systems of theology have developed only because men can't understand, to their own satisfaction, what God says. Rather than trusting God, people try by human wisdom to explain God's words away.

The Preacher of Ecclesiastes wrote that although earthly wisdom is vain, the futility of it in the end may drive us closer to God. Sooner or later, human wisdom will run dry. Captivated by frustration and emptiness, then we may reach out to God. Earthly wisdom is really part of a

*The Foolishness
of Wisdom*

great means by which God humbles fallen man and prepares the way for his redemption. When man is humiliated in the futility of his ingenuity, God is able to bring him to himself.

"For God gives those who please him wisdom, knowledge, and joy" (2:26). All other wisdom is vanity, frustration, grief, increasing pain. The person who begins his quest for knowledge with a basic trust in God is given wisdom and joy. Every energy of the man who departs from God ends in vanity and foolishness.

This is not to say that a man who strives after knowledge and wisdom won't find it, because he will. God wants us to do everything we can to gain understanding. But we have a choice as to whether we will seek wisdom and knowledge with joy, or wisdom and knowledge with grief. It brings us to see again how much we need God.

3
Living for Pleasure
Ecclesiastes 2:1-3

"I SAID IN MINE HEART, Go to now, I will prove thee with mirth, therefore enjoy pleasure: and, behold, this also is vanity. I said of laughter, It is mad: and of mirth, What doeth it?" (2:1-3, KJV).

Ecclesiastes investigates every avenue of human endeavor, to search out everything that is done under the sun. The Preacher has discussed various things that men say would make them happy or lead to fulfillment. Next, he examines pleasure as the avenue of happiness.

Some people say that to be happy they need only to satisfy all their appetites. We are often admonished to make pleasure the chief end of life. Our urges tell us to live only for now, forsaking duty and reason. If it feels good, do it!

Seeking pleasure involves delighting the senses—sight, taste, smell, touch, and hearing. But is there any real happiness or satisfaction in this kind of pursuit? All of us, to one extent or another, are involved in the pursuit, because pleasure is a valuable part of life.

THE SCOPE OF PLEASURE

The Preacher pointed out three truths about pleasure. First he described its scope and the different kinds, all of which he tried to engage in. He spoke of laughter, mirth, or merriment (2:1). Elsewhere he talked about the laughter of a fool who disregards God and he pointed out the futility of that (7:6). Amusement—doing those things that make us laugh—gives pleasure. He spoke of unrestrained merriment, mirth-making, being entertained. No society has been more characterized by its insatiable hunger for amusement than ours. The Preacher was not trying to make hermits out of us, nor was he suggesting that when we make amusement and pleasure the chief goals in life, we will find that they cannot deliver what we are trying to get from them. We need times of relaxation, times of withdrawal and re-creation. But to make these the chief end of life is futile.

We in America have gone amusement mad. Many are far more distressed over the current status of our favorite football team than about our community and the unsaved of the world. Many are more interested in being entertained than in being involved in the democratic process of our land. We don't want to be bothered; we want to be amused. We think if we can be involved in enough distractions, we can forget the real world and everything will be all right. The writer of Ecclesiastes said, "I have tried that."

Next, he talked about alcohol (2:3). He decided to see what controlled drinking could do for him. Obviously he was not talking about drunkenness or excessive drinking, but about the temperate use of wine to bring out the best in him, to stimulate his body. But that too was futile. "Then I decided to spend my time having fun, because I felt that there was nothing better in all the earth than that a man should eat, drink, and be merry, with the hope that this happiness would stick with him in all the hard work which God gives to mankind everywhere" (8:15).

When we have commended pleasure to its fullest, we still cannot make sense out of life. "Only God can see everything, and even the wisest man who says he knows everything, doesn't" (8:17). A man who lives without God and makes pleasure the end of his life, though he may say, "I have found the answer," has failed.

Everything that affluence could bring, the Preacher tried. It was all a part of his search and testing of pleasure.

The human achievements of the writer of Ecclesiastes were staggering. It is nice to win—to succeed in life. It is good to reach goals, but after we have taken pleasure in reaching the goals, it all boils down to emptiness. It feels good to work hard and to achieve something, but if our achievements simply feed our desire for display, or to be recognized for vain show, they don't bring ultimate satisfaction.

Whatever his senses desired to experience, he pursued. He gave himself to the sensual pleasures of this earth. "I searched everywhere, determined to find wisdom and the reason for things, and to prove to myself the wickedness of folly, and that foolishness is madness. A prostitute is more bitter than death. May it please God that you escape from her, but sinners don't evade her snares" (7:25, 26). So he tried even the sensual, immoral sins of society. We today are living in a world that tells us that if we satisfy our sensual desires, we will be happy. Consequently, we have become one of the most immoral, dishonest, overweight generations that has ever existed.

THE SYSTEM OF PLEASURE

Second, notice the system of pleasure, how he did not recklessly plunge into it. His approach sounded like a form of scientific investigation. He was really using wisdom as the key to his search. He was not a person filled with a passion for lust, success, or any worldly achievement. He carefully examined things to see if there really was pleasure in anything the world had to offer. "So after a lot of thinking, I decided to try the road of drink, while still holding steadily to my course of seeking wisdom" (2:3). "And with it all I remained clear-eyed" (2:9).

We are being told today that it is all right to drink as long as we don't drink a lot. When the writer of Ecclesiastes wisely tried it, he found it was vain. We are told it is all right to be dishonest as long as we don't get caught and aren't too involved. We are told it is all right to be immoral as long as we are discreet. But the Preacher tried it all with all wisdom, with full control of his lusts. He didn't go headlong into evil in such a way as to destroy himself. Carefully, he tried it all as wisely as it is humanly possible for anyone to pursue pleasure. He was not excessive or abusive, but careful and objective. "And I applied myself to search for understanding about everything in the universe" (1:13).

His test was not conducted because of his love of pleasure but from a real desire to find out if pleasure held any lasting answers, any lasting satisfaction. Laughter and pleasure are legitimate expressions. He was not talking about ungodly pleasure, but about the legitimate expression of things that might be quite proper in their place. He was saying, however, that when he investigated, he found that these things do not satisfy. It is all right to laugh and to have joy in life, but if we count on that for lasting fulfillment, we will be sadly disillusioned.

THE SATISFACTION OF PLEASURE

The Preacher discussed the *scope* of his search, the *system* of his search, and the *satisfaction* of it. His pursuit of pleasure was intellectual, proper, and systematic. "But as I looked at everything I had tried, it was all so useless, a chasing of the wind, and there was nothing really worth-

*Ecclesiastes
2:1-3*

while anywhere" (2:11). He wanted to see if man could find satisfaction and lasting happiness, meaning, and purpose in life in the things that simply satisfy his cravings. The conclusion was that it was all vanity. Paul wrote later: "But she that liveth in pleasure is dead while she liveth" (1 Tim. 5:6, KJV). There is no lasting satisfaction in earthly pleasure.

The pleasure-seekers of this life first experience feasting, then famine. First they bloat themselves and then they hate themselves for their excesses. They live it up and then have to live it down. They are rich, then poor; they laugh, then they weep. But for God's children, it is just the opposite of that. The poor become rich. The lowly shall be exalted; they that sow in tears shall reap in joy. Those who mourn shall be comforted. Those who suffer with Christ will reign with him. The vanity of wearing ourselves out in pursuit of pleasure is that when the enjoyment is over, only a feeling of emptiness is left behind. When all the excitement is gone, when the passion has been satisfied, there is nothing left.

Such a pursuit of pleasure impairs our understanding, for we find that we must constantly be devising new ways and means of pleasure. What pleases us today will not satisfy tomorrow. Sin leads to greater sin. Pleasure leads to a larger pleasure. We think we will find satisfaction but our appetite increases and leads to something else. We reach a plateau, and think that if we could just reach the next level we would find the satisfaction for which we search.

Our hearts become hard, cold, and cynical. When we make pleasure our chief aim, we become enslaved, trapped by that which we sought to enjoy. We wanted to be the master but we end up being the slave. And, more serious, our conscience becomes blunt, seared in our pursuit of pleasure.

Where does it all end? The Preacher wrote: "I said in

mine heart, Go to now, I will prove thee with mirth, therefore enjoy pleasure: and, behold, this also is vanity. I said of laughter, It is mad: and of mirth, What doeth it?" (2:1, 2, KJV). When pleasure is pursued, it ends in madness. Reckless pursuit of pleasure leaves delusion, disgust, and deception.

The Preacher was not trying to make us dull, unhappy people. There is nothing wrong with pulling for our favorite football team, if we don't let it determine whether or not we will digest our food well or sleep well that night. There is nothing wrong with recreation, leisure activity, but such must not be our god and become more important to us than doing what God wants us to do. There is nothing wrong with enjoyment, laughter, pleasure found in a job well done, but it must not be our main pursuit of life. As we give ourselves to God, the enjoyment and pleasures of life will have meaning. But they will always be subservient to him. He will be the goal and the direction of our lives.

In a sensate culture where we all want to know how it feels, how it tastes, how it looks, we need to realize that there is more to life than what we can sense with our bodies. If we are to have the satisfaction of those senses, there needs to be a relationship with God that will lead us to their enjoyment.

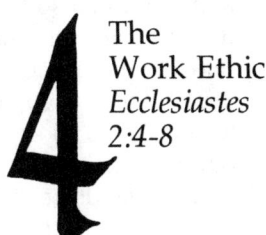

4
The Work Ethic
Ecclesiastes 2:4-8

SINCE WISDOM AND KNOWLEDGE brought no satisfaction, the Preacher turned to another activity—work. There is nothing wrong with working hard, with trying to be an achiever, to be somebody, to do something worthwhile, to make a mark in the world. But bear in mind that the writer of Ecclesiastes is dealing with the philosophy that says, "We can make life work and we can make life meaningful without God."

As the Preacher discovered, wisdom is a good pursuit, but the best man's mind can develop brings no lasting satisfaction. He learned also that seeking personal pleasure didn't really satisfy. Will personal endeavor and toil fare any better?

The Preacher continued: "I made me great works; I builded me great houses; I planted me vineyards: I made me gardens and orchards, and I planted trees in them of all kind of fruits: I made me pools of water, to water therewith the wood that bringeth forth trees: I got me servants and maidens, and had servants born in my house; also I had great possessions of great and small cattle above all that were in Jerusalem before me: I gathered me also silver and gold, and the peculiar treasure of kings and of the provinces: I got me men singers and women singers, and the delights of the sons of men, as musical instruments, and that of all sorts. So I was great, and increased more than all that were before me in Jerusalem: also my wisdom remained with me. And whatsoever mine eyes desired I kept not from them, I withheld not my heart from any joy; for my heart rejoiced in all my labour: and this was my portion of all my labour. Then I looked on all the works that my hands had wrought, and on the labour that I had laboured to do: and, behold, all was vanity and vexation of spirit, and there was no profit under the sun" (2:4-11, KJV).

Everything he did, he did for himself in the energy of the flesh. The Preacher concluded that without God all our diligence is unable to bring lasting meaning and reaches no worthy goal.

DILIGENCE COMMENDED

Four truths are taught about the effort of work. First, he commended diligence (11:6-8). A person has to venture if he wants to be successful. A man that always checks the wind, that always waits for the ideal day to plant seed, will never plant. If we don't have a faith bold enough to venture out, we will not achieve anything.

Two examples of diligence are given—the wind and the tree. The wind keeps blowing and we don't know where it comes from or where it is going, nor can we control it or predict it very accurately. A tree falls to the ground wherever it will. If it falls to the south, it lies fallen to the south. The truth is it did not consult anyone about where it would be convenient for it to fall. It just fell. So, if we wait for the "might-have-beens" and the "maybes," if we wait for a time that we can predict and control, we will never venture out. The writer of Ecclesiastes gives a real commendation to the energetic, adventuresome person who endeavors to make things happen. Few enterprises in the world would have come about if people waited for ideal conditions before they started. And neither should we.

Second, the diligent man will be sustained by the knowledge that he has been diligent. "In the morning sow your seed, in the evening, hold not your hand. Thou knowest not whether shall prosper, either this or that, whether they both shall be alike good. Truly the light is sweet, and a pleasant thing it is for the eyes to behold the sun: but if a man live many years, and rejoice in them all; yet let him remember the days of darkness: for they shall be many. All that cometh is vanity" (11:6-8, KJV). There will be dark days, but if we have been diligent, that knowledge will sustain us in the days when the darkness comes about us. This whole passage speaks of unremitting activity. "In the morning sow your seed and in the evening withhold not your hand" (11:6), literally ought to read, "in the morning sow your seed and *unto* the evening withhold not your hand." In other words, from early morning until late evening we are to be at the job, at the task.

The Preacher concluded that even though we are diligent in earthly labors, a commendable effort, if we labor without God, everything is vain.

DISCIPLINE REWARDED

Discipline and diligence have their rewards. "Anything I wanted, I took, and did not restrain myself from any joy. I even found great pleasure in hard work. This pleasure was, indeed, my only reward for all my labors" (2:10). "There was nothing better for a man to do than to enjoy his food and drink, and his job. Then I realized that even this pleasure is from the hand of God" (2:24).

There is something satisfying and rewarding about being disciplined and creative. The ability to manage a great establishment, the ability to create dreams and ideas

The Work Ethic

is sweet and good. What spoils these basic pursuits of life is our passion to get more out of them than they can give. We do not seem to understand their limitations. The works of our hands can never give us ultimate satisfaction. Even the joy of creativity soon wears out. The pleasure disappears when the dream is achieved.

A young wrestler, after he won the gold medal in the Olympics, told of how he had given his whole life to become an Olympic gold medal wrestling champion, to be the best in the world in his weight division. With a tinge of sadness he said, "As I stood on the top step with the gold medallion about my neck, and as they played "The Star-Spangled Banner," I suddenly understood that everything I had given my life to achieve was behind me. For years I had worked and now all my work was over."

The reward and joy in creativity lasts only as long as the project lasts. Afterward, there remains a hunger in the heart for something else. The author wrote: "Well, one thing at least is good: it is for a man to eat well, drink a good glass of wine, accept his position in life, and enjoy his work whatever his job may be, for however long the Lord may let him live. And, of course, it is very good if a man has received wealth from the Lord, and the good health to enjoy it. To enjoy your work and to accept your lot in life—that is indeed a gift from God" (5:18-20). He did not say that wealth is the gift of God, but the ability to enjoy life and use wisely that which God gives us through our efforts is truly the gift of God. The tragedy is that most people cannot stand success. Few men hold their wealth under their power. Most of them stand under the power of their wealth—driven by it, dominated by it. Only God can give us the gift of truly enjoying the works of our hand.

We have a way of forgetting the good days. "For he shall not much remember the days of his life: because God answereth him in the joy of his heart" (5:20, KJV). We don't remember the days that the sun shines. But we will remember the day the tornado blows through town. We seem to have the ability to forget the good and to remember only the bad. However, the book of Ecclesiastes does say that the man who is diligent and who disciplines himself can be satisfied with his labor, if he understands what he might rightfully expect from it.

DISTINCTION ACHIEVED

Ecclesiastes shows that diligence is commended, discipline is rewarded, and distinction can be achieved in this life. The writer was evidently a successful businessman (2:4-6), distinguished for his achievements. His financial rewards were great (2:7, 8). He had money in the bank. He had servants—everything that such luxury could give. "So I became greater than any of the kings in Jerusalem before me and with it all I remained clear-eyed, so that I could evaluate all these things" (2:9). His brilliance was recognized. He was a man of distinction.

It is possible for us in this life, with the effort of our hands and the energy of our lives, to achieve, to build, to reap some of the fruit and joy of our labor, to enjoy the satisfaction and acclaim of good hard work, and still, looking back over it all, to say, "It was futile, empty!"

DISTRESS RECEIVED

In the midst of this diligence, discipline, and distinction, there was distress. "But as I looked at everything I had tried, it was all so useless, a chasing of the wind, and there was nothing really worthwhile anywhere" (2:11). "For God giveth to a man that is good in his sight wisdom, and knowledge, and joy: but to the sinner he giveth travail, to gather and to heap up, that he may give to him that is good before God. This also is vanity and vexation of spirit" (2:26, KJV).

For us to call the things we achieve with our hands eternal is pure fantasy and foolishness. Nothing perishable will ever satisfy our hearts. If we translate "there is no profit under the sun" (2:11, KJV) into our vernacular, we would say, "It doesn't mean a thing. It is like chasing the wind." When we take a backward look, everything we have undertaken is extremely disappointing. Without God, even honest work is futile.

Good honest labor can sometimes produce envy and a competitive spirit. "Then I observed that the basic motive for success is the driving force of envy and jealousy!" (4:4). Hard work is often mixed with a craving to outshine someone else. Friendly rivalry plays a bigger part in our work for God than we would like to admit. Resentments are often nursed. Grievances are often held as a result. A jealous or envious spirit destroys much of the joy of success. If we are not careful, no matter what we achieve, we will be so jealous of the person who achieves more that we won't enjoy what we have. There will always be somebody to top whatever we do. What we do can be simply for show, simply so that people will praise us, if we aren't careful. This is in itself a distress to avoid.

A third distress is often called "the rat race," or the "vicious cycle," or the "workaholic syndrome." "Wise men and fools alike spend their lives scratching for food, and never seem to get enough" (6:7). Searching for food and never being satisfied is a vicious cycle. "Better is the sight of the eyes than the wandering of the desire" (6:9, KJV). Desire drives a man on and on to achieve, yet he is never satisfied, never able to rest. However plentiful satisfaction of fleshly appetites may be, there is always a longing for something else. The hunger in the soul of man gives no rest. We are reminded here that a man's mouth or his physical gratification and not his mind is his master.

Ecclesiastes 2:4-8

The compulsive moneymaker doesn't have time to sleep. He is always on the move, striving, always reaching for something else. "In my search for wisdom I observed all that was going on everywhere across the earth—ceaseless activity, day and night" (8:16). "Days full of sorrow and grief and restless, bitter nights" (2:23). These verses picture a man driven on and virtually dehumanized. He has surrendered to the craving and the endless process of feeding his desire.

"I also observed another piece of foolishness around the earth. This is the case of a man who is quite alone, without a son or brother, yet he works hard to keep gaining more riches and to whom will he leave it all? And why is he giving up so much now? It is all so pointless and depressing" (4:7, 8). Here is a picture of a man driven by his job, who has no time for anything or anyone else. If he has a family, he gives them money, provides the physical things, but has no time for them. His god, the master of his life, is his job. He has no meaningful relationships, neither brother, son, nor family. His vicious cycle is one of the distresses of the work ethic. The Preacher of Ecclesiastes showed that no amount of labor to accumulate perishable things can satisfy.

The worst distress of all is found in the next verses. After the man has given his life to achieve, he has to turn everything over to someone else. "And I am disgusted about this, that I must leave the fruits of all my hard work to others. And who can tell whether my son will be a wise man or a fool? And yet all I have will be given to him—how discouraging! So I turned in despair from hard work as the answer to my search for satisfaction. For though I spend my life searching for wisdom, knowledge, and skill, I must leave all of it to someone who hasn't done a day's work in his life; he inherits all my efforts, free of charge. This is not only foolish, but unfair" (2:18-21).

When we have built what we can build with our hands,

someone else gets it. It is frustrating to see that which we have labored for slip from our control, but sooner or later, it has to happen. It is disappointing to watch the things which one toiled for disintegrate in the hands of another. But that is the endless process of life, apart from God.

All that is done under the sun is vain. Only God can lift toil and labor from being futile to being eternal. Only God can translate effort and energy into fulfillment. We are told to be energetic and creative. We are told to do a good job, to gain satisfaction and joy from being the very best we can. But only God can take what we produce and translate it into eternal blessing.

Even for the man who has planned and built the best he could, all his travail becomes grief. "For all his days are sorrows and his travail grief; yea, his heart taketh not rest in the night" (2:23, KJV).

"The fool won't work and almost starves, but feels that it is better to be lazy and barely get by, than to work hard when, in the long run, it is all so futile" (4:5). Both the hard worker and the lazy man are extremes, but they are both disappointing. The Preacher was not praising the fool. He was just saying that if we do not allow God into our lives to give our desires and achievements meaning and permanence, then we are the greatest fools of all.

We must commit the efforts of our flesh and the energies of our lives to him. If, for example, we are students, we should study hard and make the best possible grades.

We ought to build the finest businesses in the world. The most excellent professions should be led by Christians. We should be the best. But if we have done it all in our energy, the work ethic will not give us joy and peace. The ethic that says "Work hard and get what you can" will not satisfy. Only God can.

Whatever we do, we must do it as unto the Lord. By doing so, we will be laying up treasures in heaven. We will be doing the very best we can for our employer—for those

Ecclesiastes 2:4-8

to whom we are responsible—when we are doing it as unto God. God will reward us. We may have unjust supervisors. But by being fair to them and giving our best to them because we are doing it as unto the Lord, God can still reward us and our work.

The choice is ours. We can build with our hands, labor with our energies, and do it unto God, letting him lay hold to the work of time, transferring it into work for eternity. Or we can work in our own energy and lose even the joy and satisfaction that comes from that work.

5

The Success Syndrome
Ecclesiastes 2:9-11

ACHIEVING SUCCESS and recognition are probably the most common ways that men through the years have sought to find happiness. The Preacher concluded, after he had described all of the energy he had put forth in building a great empire, "So I was great, and increased more than all that were before me in Jerusalem: also my wisdom remained with me. And whatsoever mine eyes desired I kept not from them, I withheld not my heart from any joy; for my heart rejoiced in all my labour: and this was my portion of all my labour. Then I looked on all the works that my hands had wrought, and on the labour that I had laboured to do: and, behold, all was vanity and vexation of the spirit, and there was no profit under the sun" (2:9-11, KJV).

PASSION FOR RECOGNITION

In every man's heart is the passion for recognition. The common experience of mankind is that nobody wants to be a nobody. A basic personality drive of everyone is the desire for life to have meaning, to feel that one has achieved something, to feel his achievements have been properly recognized and praised.

Ecclesiastes 2:9-11

The writer pointed out that within his heart also there was a passion for recognition and achievement. He was voicing what is common to all of us. Conversely, if we don't reach the achievement we desire, we feel we are less than somebody.

But here is a fallacy. Most people feel and believe, however subconsciously, that the greatness of their achievements is somehow transferred to themselves so that their personal value is measured by their achievements. In other words, if we achieve something, we will be important; but if we don't, we won't be. It is the belief that makes us want to excel.

This desire is not all bad. Everyone of us ought to want to excel. The Christian call is a call to excellence, to be significant in this world. But it is an excellence not to be based upon human energy. It is the outworking of the power of God through us.

We are to excel, we are to be different, we are to have lives that reflect the glory of God. But it is God moving through us that makes such a life possible. The writer of Ecclesiastes pointed out the arrogance, self-confidence, and self-sufficiency that usually accompanies this passion for recognition. "It is better to be a poor but wise youth than to be an old and foolish king who refuses all advice. Such a lad could come from prison and succeed. He might even become king, though born in poverty. Everyone is eager to help a youth like that, even to help him usurp the throne. He can become the leader of millions of people, and be very popular. But, then, the younger generation grows up around him and rejects him! So again, it is all foolishness, chasing the wind" (4:13-16).

The writer described here a man who achieved the recognition of being the king. He had been around a long time. The more he was around, the more tenaciously he held to the honor and prestige he had, oblivious to the counsel and advice of others. He was so caught up in what he had achieved that he thought he knew it all. With self-sufficiency and arrogance, he pushed everyone else aside. He was proud and stubborn and lost his perspective and courtesy. He would have done anything to succeed. That is the kind of passion that is inside us that drives us on.

We see it every day. It is true in school. Why do girls want to be cheerleaders? Is it to help the team win? Of course not—they want the recognition, which is basic to athletics. A football player wants to be a great quarterback, not necessarily because he wants the team to win, but because he wants to be recognized as a great quarterback.

We would be surprised how much selfishness, arrogance, and stubbornness there is in our passion for recognition. There is seldom in us the magnanimous spirit that says, "I am going to work hard, do the job, and know that I have done a job well. And just knowing that I did it is sufficient reward. I do not care if I am recognized or not." It would be exciting to have a church full of people like that. How much we could get done if nobody cared who got credit for it! But there is a basic passion to achieve, to be recognized.

Why does a man drive himself to be the best in his business, to do more business than anyone else? Is it so he can make a contribution to the national economy? I doubt it! I once counseled at length with a multimillionaire. He already had more money in the bank than he could spend in a dozen lifetimes. He said, "I have to succeed. I have to be the biggest and the best in the whole world at what I am doing." Why? His answer: "I have to. There is something in me that says I have to be on the top. The money is not important, but I have to be the one who succeeds over everyone else."

All of us face this passion in one way or another. The severity of the temptations of Jesus was not to get him to do something unlawful, but to get him to do something proper in the wrong way. The passion to succeed is a

*Ecclesiastes
2:9-11*

basic and good desire of our hearts. But it is very hard for us to maintain a right spirit as we go about it.

THE PERIL OF RECOGNITION

There are many perils and pitfalls along the way in achieving recognition for ourselves. When we have achieved it, what do we have? It is like a small child at a fair. When the child is offered a choice between a big, colorful, fluffy cotton candy ball, or a stick of candy, he will probably choose the cotton candy. It is bigger and prettier. But what is cotton candy but a tiny portion of spun sugar? If the child knew how very little the portion was, he might not want to buy it, but the truth is, he doesn't really know what he has and isn't even sure he has eaten it after it is gone, it was so light.

There are pitfalls to recognition. What does recognition give us? What do we get when we are elected to be cheerleader, become first string quarterback, or the top man in our field in the world?

The writer of Ecclesiastes described a man who came out of obscurity to become king. After he had achieved his stature, someone else came out of obscurity and took his place. Before long, he will be back at the bottom and the person he never heard of will be on top. This emphasizes the uncertainty and the insecurity of success. When we get it, we can't keep it. Today we may receive recognition for a certain achievement, but next year there will be someone else, and twenty years from now, no one will even remember our names. Jesus said in the Sermon on the Mount that if we go about bragging about our prayers and gifts, we receive our reward in that recognition. But that is all we receive.

Only fleeting honors come to worldly recognition. Time soon passes us by. A man reaches the pinnacle of human glory only to be stranded there. "There is no end to all the people, even of all that have been before them: they also that come after shall not rejoice in him" (4:16, KJV). Succeeding generations will not remember him at all. Human adulation and adoration are fickle. People who praise us will curse us just as quickly. What do we do after we reach the top? We can't climb any higher than that. The acclaim and recognition are so short-lived that they are certainly not worth building our lives upon.

THE PRICE OF RECOGNITION
If we are going to get worldly recognition, there is a price we must pay. "Anything I wanted, I took, and did not restrain myself from any joy. I even found great pleasure in hard work. This was, indeed, my only reward for all my labors. But as I looked at everything I had tried, it was all so useless, a chasing of the wind, and there was nothing really worthwhile anywhere" (2:10, 11). The first price to pay is the satisfaction that turns sour. The joy vanishes when the new wears off. Whatever we have, we want something else once the newness is gone. Because of our insatiable hunger for the novel, we aren't ever satisfied.

Politicians in every state in the union and in the Senate and Congress are often people of high standing and great financial resources. They are in politics for one reason—they set out for worldly recognition and achievement, and when they reached the level of financial success, they wanted something more, so they kept pressing on, thinking when they reached the next goal of political success, they would find satisfaction. They don't realize that their satisfaction soon wears off. This is the price of recognition. Those who see it at all costs will never find the peace they search for.

"God has given to some men very great wealth and

Ecclesiastes 2:9-11

honor, so that they can have everything they want, but he doesn't give them the health to enjoy it, and they die and others get it all! This is absurd, a hollow mockery, and a serious fault" (6:2). Here is a man who reaches the top but can't enjoy it. Many times God withholds from successful people the gift to benefit from and enjoy their achievements. We all know of people who seem to have everything turn out right for them. But God says, "It may appear that they have everything going their way, that they have everything their hearts desire, but I will not give them the power to eat thereof, the power to enjoy it. What they have will never satisfy."

All the acclaim that men dream of still can leave them unfulfilled and empty inside. The Preacher warned those who seem to prosper when they are evil and declared that they will not have the power to be satisfied with what they get. It is a price one pays for worldly recognition. Some young people sell their souls to be recognized. Parents sell their children's souls so that their offspring can be recognized and the parents have vicarious recognition. Some parents vicariously live through their children, reaching goal after goal after goal, but are never satisfied. If you don't believe that, go out to the soccer field or the baseball field someday and watch a Little League game. Seldom is there trouble from the children or the coaches. It is the parents who scream the loudest if their son doesn't make the right play.

It is sad that we are such a goal-oriented society. Recognition that comes through God is the only kind that will endure. Very few of the students adulated in high school and college ever achieve real distinction later in life. It is because they are caught up on the recognition factor and never are satisfied, pressing on and on for the wrong reasons. Because they have no time for God and his counsel, they never find real happiness. But the man who recognizes his sin, his inability, that he is nobody, is a man in whose life God can move and make to be somebody, with eternal values and rewards.

"No man can hold back his spirit from departing; no one has the power to prevent his day of death, for there is no discharge from that obligation and that dark battle. Certainly a man's wickedness is not going to help him then. I have thought deeply about all that goes on here in the world, where people have the power of injuring each other. I have seen wicked men buried and their friends returned from the cemetery, having forgotten all the dead man's evil deeds, these men were praised in the very city where they had committed their many crimes! How odd! Because God does not punish sinners instantly, people feel it is safe to do wrong. But though a man sins a hundred times and still lives, I know very well that those who fear God will be better off, unlike the wicked, who will not live long, good lives—their days shall pass away as quickly as shadows because they don't fear God" (8:8-13).

What difference does it make whether the wicked live their span of life longer and seem to obtain recognition more than the humble and more than the righteous? What difference does it make when we place it beside the standard of eternity? God says, "They won't prolong their days."

Somehow, we must understand that truth and determine where our priorities lie. Will we give ourselves to do that which we cannot keep? Will we give ourselves to that which is quickly forgotten? Or will we give ourselves to that which is eternal, that which will bring meaning and purpose to life?

I heard years ago of a missionary who had been in the Orient many years. Because he had been there a long time, and because he knew the people, he became well accepted among the leaders of that nation. A major oil company approached him about representing them in the Orient. They sent a representative from this country where he was

Ecclesiastes 2:9-11

serving to ask him if he would agree to represent them. In return, they would pay him well with a wonderful place to live and a great position of respect and authority over the entire area. He refused. They kept coming back with unbelievable financial offers but this man, committed to eternal ideals, finally convinced them he would not do it. He said of their offer, "The pay is big, but the job is small."

Throughout life, that is our choice. We may be offered some large paying jobs, acclaim, and recognition. We may be tempted to sell our souls for the great praise and acclaim that men give us. We must remember when that offer comes that although the pay may seem big, the rewards may be small. Recognition does not last if it is earned in human energy. Only that which is committed to Christ endures.

The Tyranny of Time
Ecclesiastes 3:1-9

6

TO THINK of chapter three of Ecclesiastes as expressing the tyranny of time might seem inappropriate. We see, in glancing through this passage, a gentle ebb and flow: a time for this, and a time for that. A time to plant seed, a time to harvest the crop. At first it seems as tranquil as a lullaby, rocking us to sleep. But there is something frustrating in the gentleness, something distressing about that movement back and forth. As we read through it, something reaches out, at least subconsciously, to say that even this gentle ebb and flow, this emphasis on the proper season for things to do is really no more fulfilling than the endless circle and the rat race of life that has already been carefully projected.

We like rhythm and variety. We like for things to be systematic. But even that offers no lasting satisfaction to our hearts. Many people, I believe, have misunderstood this passage of Scripture. Most have understood it to say that there is a proper time for everything that man can do. Thus, if we are very intelligent, we will pick the right time to do the right thing. But that interpretation is not accurate. We can't choose a time to do certain things. Rather, the times are chosen for us. Who chooses when to be born? Certainly not us. Who chooses when to die? Certainly that is beyond our discretion. This passage speaks of the tyranny of time, of the fact that time has dominion over us. Something controls our actions and actually designates what we will face. We do not usually choose the things that we face in life but rather those things are brought to us by an unseen force, beyond our comprehension.

The Preacher raised some important truths for our consideration. We are bound by time, in some way—victims of it. God stood in eternity, before there was time, and created man. In the eternity that shall extend beyond time, we will not be victimized by time. We don't first get old and then become young. There is a chronological factor about life and to face it we must abide by it and live with it.

WE DON'T WRITE THE RULES
First, we live by rules not of our own choosing. Whatever else this passage says, it reminds us that we don't have the opportunity to decide what we are going to face in life. Any individual who does not have an alternate action, who does not learn to live with life's second choices, will never understand life at all. We must have a game plan for disappointment, realizing that we have no control over time.

However much we may dislike our existence, we have to live with it. It does not matter how much we might have liked to have gone west in a covered wagon, we will never have the opportunity. We are living now. We are living by rules over which we have no choice. "Even if a man has a hundred sons and as many daughters and lives to be very old, but leaves so little money at his death that his children can't even give him a decent burial—I say that he would be better off born dead" (6:3). The length of life—the span of years—does not bring fulfillment in itself.

THIS LIFE HAS NO PERMANENCE
Second, nothing we pursue in this life has any real permanence. The writer of Ecclesiastes, remember, was talking about life "under the sun." Nothing we pursue apart from God has any permanence. We are always chasing rainbows, gathering dewdrops, building castles in the sand. "I know that there is no good in them, but for a man to rejoice and to do good in his life" (3:12, KJV). The phrase "in his life" casts a shadow over everything we do. There is a limit to what we can achieve.

In the framework of time, there is no permanence and nothing that we pursue has lasting value. Change is inevitable. We have little to say about the situations that move us to weep, or to laugh, or to mourn. Which one of us sits down and decides to have a pathetic cry?

There is a time to be born, a time to die, a time to plant, a time to harvest. Most of the situations which move us into these activities are beyond our control.

What are we to do about it? We have to make the best of it. The lost man and the saved man have the same need to make the best of the time each has. The difference is that the lost man has no ability to make the best of it. He works in a void, a vacuum. He works unaware that over all of life there is the guiding hand of a benevolent, loving, compassionate, concerned God who has provided time, life, and circumstances for us. It is all within the framework of his presence, his will, and his purpose. Time no longer holds tyranny over the believer. It no longer pressures him and dominates him, but releases him to find fulfillment in the midst of a transitional world.

TIME IS NOT HAPHAZARD
Third, time is not haphazard. Apart from God, we pursue that which is temporary and changeable. But behind it all,

Ecclesiastes 3:1-9

there is God. Time doesn't have to be a vicious enemy which robs us of our youth, strength, and vitality, for every circumstance of time is in the hand of God. The answer is not for us to find a place where there is no change, or to try to find a consistency that is not affected by time, but to find order and purpose in the midst of change and time.

This passage means that there is a time for God to do all things. This passage refers to him and not to us, for obviously we cannot choose the time of our birth and death. It is God's activities we are talking about. When he says there is a time to be born and a time to die, he is talking about God's time, God's moving, God's purpose.

The Preacher was speaking in this passage about fourteen different kinds of activities of God in this world. The circumstances of life, however vicious or surprising they may seem to be, are really gracious gifts from the hand of a benevolent God. So we face the uncertainties of life, the tyranny of time, knowing that God is behind it all. God will make all things work together for good because we love him and are called according to his purpose. We move into time and the uncertainties that are before us knowing that God is there. We do not live our lives victimized by chance or fate, concerned about what Mother Nature is going to do. We live, guided by the hand of our sovereign God. It is a beautiful picture.

Such guidance takes all the pressure off us. Real success requires God's guidance. We cannot understand it, but it is not for us to try to figure out how to do the right thing at the right time. We might laugh when we should weep. We might do what is right at the wrong time. It is not for us to try to plan how to find a season for all these things. Our responsibility is to trust God, to let him do his work. The last portion of this passage explains that we could never understand God. "He hath made everything beautiful in his time: also he hath set the world in their

The Tyranny of Time

heart, so that no man can find out the work that God maketh from the beginning to the end" (3:11, KJV).

No one understands the future but God. The unfathomable truth of an eternal God who moves in mysterious ways among his people, who often do not recognize his authority or his existence, is the emphasis of these verses. Through it all, God moves the world to an inevitable climax when his purposes are achieved.

Our obedience and worship of God open the door for meaning in our time-bound lives. We can never understand the apparent inequities or the tragedies of life. All the things we might change about our lives only perplex us. We cannot understand the seeming dominance of evil, the mystery of war, the tragedy of hate and prejudice, poverty, and malnutrition in the world that God has created. Nor can we comprehend how a God who created us in love and sent his Son to die for us could let this world go on the way it is going. We cannot comprehend because we are under the tyranny of time. We can't reach beyond time with our finite minds into eternity to see as God does.

We can choose to go blindly through life, doing what we can, reaching for whatever goals we desire, pleasing our own fancy, guided by our own wisdom. Or we can put our hands in the hand of the sovereign God who knows the past from the future. Since we don't know the future, it makes sense to trust someone who does.

We can be bound by time, or we can march victoriously, conquerors of time, through him who holds all time in his hand.

When we give ourselves to life here on earth, we are giving ourselves to that which cannot endure. But when we invest our faith, trust, and energies in him who guides the destiny of the world, we cannot fail.

7

Our Sovereign God
Ecclesiastes 3:10-18

ALTHOUGH ECCLESIASTES talks about the sovereignty of God, it does not deal with every aspect of this great theme. As with any doctrine in Scripture, a part of the truth should not be considered as if it were the whole truth. Other facets of God's sovereignty are mentioned elsewhere in Scripture.

In considering this important subject, we begin by finding the world's place in God's plan. Some wrongly have the idea that we need to find where we can fit God into our lives. The truth is that God is sovereign and our task is to find where we fit into his plan. Dr. William Bell made a very comprehensive statement about the sovereignty of God: "God has an ultimate purpose for everything that happens and the underlying purpose is to bring glory to God. Nothing happens that God does not intend to use for a specific purpose. Nothing happens that God does not intend to bring glory to Himself through that occurrence." The book of Ecclesiastes underscores these truths.

"I know that, whatsoever God doeth, it shall be for ever; nothing can be put to it, nor anything taken from it: and God doeth it, that men should fear before him. That which hath been is now; and that which is to be hath already been; and God requireth that which is past. And moreover I saw under the sun the place of judgment, that wickedness was there; and the place of righteousness, that iniquity was there. I said in mine heart, God shall judge the righteous and the wicked: for there is a time there for every purpose and for every work" (3:14-17, KJV).

CREATION
The Preacher spoke of God's sovereignty as it is expressed in creation. God created man's body, he created man's spirit, and he created the world.

His sovereignty is especially seen in his creation of our physical bodies. "As thou knowest not what is the way of the spirit, nor how the bones do grow in the womb of her that is with child: even so thou knowest not the works of God who maketh all" (11:5, KJV). The most satisfying, fulfilling explanation of the origin of physical man is the creative sovereignty of God. God created every function in the body and every physical need that we have. The Preacher of Ecclesiastes declared, "Remember now thy creator in the days of thy youth" (12:1). In those tender years, before we have become hardened to sin and before we have become calloused to God's Spirit, we are to acknowledge our Creator.

There is more to man than just his physical body. God created man with a spirit. "And I found that though God had made man upright, each has turned away to follow his own downward road" (7:29). The writer, talking about much more than physical attributes, was referring to man being made in the image of God. "And the dust returns to the earth as it was, and the spirit returns to God who gave it" (12:7). Because the Spirit belongs to God, man can never find real contentment with less than what God has for him. Man's spirit can never rest until it rests in the one who created it, until it knows peace with God. When God created man as a physical being, he "breathed

Ecclesiastes 3:10-18

into his nostrils the breath of life and man became a living soul" (Gen. 2:7, KJV). Man was created an intelligent, rational, responsive, understanding person. Man's spirit makes him different from all the rest of creation.

The Preacher of Ecclesiastes reminds us that beyond the creation of the body and spirit of man, God created everything that we have. "Then I beheld all the work of God, that a man cannot find out the work that is done under the sun: because though a man labour to seek it out, yet he shall not find it: yea further: though a wise man think to know it, yet shall he not be able to find it" (8:17, KJV). The handiwork of God, the creation of this world, is beyond our full comprehension. "I gave my heart to seek and search out by wisdom concerning all things that are done under heaven" (1:13, KJV).

The Preacher calls us to "remember your Creator" (12:1). The word "remember" does not simply mean to recall, in the casual sense in which we often use it. The word used is a strong word which means to remember in such a way as to change our lives, to reshape our conduct. Since God is the Creator, he has complete and absolute claim upon us. When we remember him, we are relating to him as creature to Creator, as finite to the infinite God.

CONTROL

Another aspect of sovereignty is evidenced by God's control in the world and its destiny. "That which hath been is now; and that which is to be hath already been; and God requireth that which is past" (3:15, KJV). The little word "is" is timeless. In whatever present tense we are, there is an eternal "is." God is! The works of God are, in the continuous present tense.

God's control over the world, however, does not make us puppets on a string. It does mean everything that

*Our
Sovereign God*

comes into our lives is directed or permitted by our God who makes it best for us (Rom. 8:28). "So I decided that there was nothing better for a man to do than to enjoy his food and drink, and his job. Then I realized that even this pleasure is from the hand of God" (2:24). "And second, that he should eat and drink and enjoy the fruits of his labors, for these are gifts from God" (3:13). "Well, one thing, at least, is good: it is for a man to eat well, drink a good glass of wine, accept his position in life, and enjoy his work whatever his job may be, for however long the Lord may let him live. And, of course, it is very good if a man has received wealth from the Lord, and the good health to enjoy it. To enjoy your work and to accept your lot in life—that is indeed a gift from God. The person who does that will not need to look back with sorrow on his past, for God gives him joy" (5:18-20).

Those blessings and satisfactions that come into our lives are because of the gracious, controlling hand of God. That is a happy thought! Nothing can happen to shake me out of God's clutches. Nothing can rob me of the blessing that God intends me to have. His control extends even to all the earthly honors and wealth that we might have. God allows a man to have riches, wealth, and honor and gives him the power to enjoy what he has. It is God who not only bestows, but enables us to benefit from that which is bestowed upon us. "God has given to some men very great wealth and honor, so that they can have everything they want, but he doesn't give them the health to enjoy it, and they die and others get it all!" (6:2).

All of life bears the indelible print of God. "And I know this, that whatever God does is final—nothing can be added or taken from it; God's purpose in this is that man should fear the all-powerful God. Whatever is, has been long ago; and whatever is going to be has been before; God brings to pass again what was in the distant past

Ecclesiastes 3:10-18

and disappeared" (3:14, 15). "See the way God does things and fall into line. Don't fight the facts of nature. Enjoy prosperity whenever you can, and when hard times strike, realize that God gives one as well as the other—so that everyone will realize that nothing is certain in this life" (7:13, 14). "Then I decided to spend my time having fun, because I felt that there was nothing better in all the earth than that a man should eat, drink, and be merry, with the hope that this happiness would stick with him in all the hard work which God gives to mankind everywhere" (8:15).

For those who have given themselves to Christ, there is a wonderful awareness that all of life somehow comes under the gracious control of God. We cannot fully understand it. Natural man, who cannot understand the things of God, views with resistance and horror the thought that somehow there is a God who is in control through life. But the believer knows that he has never been loved so completely as by God. He knows that in God's great love for us, he sent his own Son to die in our behalf. He knows that God has given to us the blessings of life that transcend human understanding. To the believer it is a joy to know that in every experience of life, God is in control.

CONSIGNMENT

God is sovereign in his plan for all of our lives. Every one of us who knows that God has control of our lives can know that we are involved right now in his plan for us. There is a uniformity which God brings into our lives. Our task is to find out what God wants us to do, what he wants us to be, and then to accept it.

Many of us know what God wants, but we are not willing to do it, not ready to commit ourselves to his purpose.

His plan or consignment is not yet acceptable to us. We cannot understand how to reconcile the sovereignty of God and the responsibility of man, but it is clear that God has made us responsible beings. We possess the ability to choose as we know that he has sovereignly invested these characteristics of will in us.

If we can come to the place of accepting his will for us, we will have entered into the most blessed experience we could possibly know. His plans, unlike ours, need no corrections or amendments. They endure. "Whatsoever God doeth, it shall be forever" (3:14, KJV). God has placed eternity, something far beyond time, in our hearts and we can never be satisfied with only that which is restricted to time. God consigns us that which is eternal. Therefore, only God can bring satisfaction to the human heart.

Earthbound, natural man is a prisoner of a system he cannot break or bend, and behind it all is God. The people of God hear this truth without misgivings. The Preacher described a divine faithfulness which places the fear of God in its proper perspective (3:14). This verse does not mean we are to be scared of God, but that we are to reverence him. It means we are to worship and praise him. God's hand in our lives, God's control in our world, God's plan for our days is given to us in order to lead us to worship him. Whatever else the sovereignty of God means, it means that everything works to bring glory to God. We hear it without fear. We understand it as God being faithful when we read that he does something forever that we can't take away or add to.

We are further assured that with God all is foreknown and nothing is overlooked. "Whatever is, has been long ago; and whatever is going to be has been before; God brings to pass again what was in the distant past and disappeared" (3:15). God has no abortive enterprises and he has no forgotten people. We may think that we have

Ecclesiastes
3:10-18

failed in that enterprise for God, but if God led, we didn't fail. We may think that God has forgotten us, that the pain in our heart is so deep and so severe that God himself is not aware of it. But we are never away from the creative care of God in our lives. We are never forgotten, never turned aside, never forsaken. Jesus Christ was forsaken for us, and God turned away from him and forsook him in order to redeem us. But he never forsakes us. If we could grasp that, it would help us to say "Yes" to every directive God gives us. Here is God's plan or assignment in our lives.

CONDEMNATION

God's sovereignty is demonstrated in judgment, which will also be discussed later. God is the one who will judge the righteous and the wicked. "I said to myself, 'In due season God will judge everything man does, both good and bad' " (3:17). "Young man, it's wonderful to be young! Enjoy every minute of it! Do all you want to; take in everything, but realize that you must account to God for everything you do" (11:9). "Here is my final conclusion: fear God and obey his commandments, for this is the entire duty of man. For God will judge us for everything we do, including every hidden thing, good or bad" (12:13, 14). God judges the righteous and the wicked. His wrath is kindled when we make vows to him that we don't keep and become flippant in our worship. "In that case, your mouth is making you sin. Don't try to defend yourself by telling the messenger from God that it was all a mistake [to make a vow]. That would make God very angry; and he might destroy your prosperity" (5:6, 7).

God didn't create us and go off and leave us. Our God has a vital, personal interest in everything we do and say.

Our
Sovereign God

Through all of the crooked maze of confusion and heartache, and misunderstanding that shrouds us, there is an overriding purpose of God that all the forces of hell cannot detour. God is in control, still assigning and consigning his will in our lives. And he holds us responsible for our responses to his purpose.

8

The Inequities of Life
Ecclesiastes 4:1-3

"SO I RETURNED, and considered all the oppressions that are done under the sun: and behold the tears of such as were oppressed, and they had no comforter; and on the side of their oppressors there was power; but they had no comforter. Wherefore I praised the dead which are already dead more than the living which are yet alive. Yea, better is he than both they, which hath not yet been, who hath not seen the evil work that is done under the sun" (4:1-3, KJV).

We do not need the writer of Ecclesiastes to tell us that this is a world filled with difficulties, inequities, and gross unfairness. We have all encountered these injustices. Looking at it from another angle: "Again I looked throughout the earth and saw that the swiftest person does not always win the race, nor the strongest man the battle, and that wise men are often poor, and skillful men are not necessarily famous; but it is all by chance, by happening to be at the right place at the right time" (9:11). The man who seems best prepared to achieve the goal doesn't. The man with the best characteristics or qualities often does not achieve. Life is sometimes like that. The inequities of life find their origin in sin, in man's rebellion against the purposes of God. God had a perfect order for man. God gave to him a perfect place to live, but rebellion came in, and out of man's sinful rebellion have grown the inequities he now has to live with.

Inequity, oppression, injustice are all part of God's proving process in life. While God is not the origin of them, he uses them to accomplish his purposes in our lives. None of us has a choice about whether we will experience them. Every one of us will come to situations and will say, "This isn't right. This just isn't fair." Such an experience of injustice and inequity is a proving process for us. If we are insincere, it will become rapidly evident that we are. If we have a shallow faith, it will readily reveal itself. Faith is not what it ought to be if it goes to pieces on the rocks of oppression. Our relationship with God is not sturdy if it falls apart every time we are faced with something unjust or unfair.

The opposite is also true. A person's genuine mettle will be revealed in these times of injustice. The test of character is not how we stand success, but how we act when we ought to have and didn't or when we are unfairly treated.

PRODUCT OF UNREGENERATE HEARTS

Injustice and inequity are products of the unregenerate heart. We know that God is just, which means there could never be anything that is not perfectly right with him. He cannot be inequitable or unjust. Injustice does not find its origin in God, but in man's rebellion against God.

"And then I realized that God is letting the world go on its sinful way so that he can test mankind, and so that men themselves will see that they are no better than the beasts. For men and animals both breathe the same air, and both die. So mankind has no real advantage over the beasts; what an absurdity!" (3:18, 19). Though man is an infinite creation, if he does not have the touch of God upon his life, there is little to separate him from the beasts. He will be oppressive, unjust, hateful, and violent. He is little more than a beast without God. The Apostle Paul wrote: "I am persuaded that in my flesh dwelleth no good thing" (Rom. 7:18, KJV).

We may want to say, "Come on, Paul. There has to be something good in you." Paul said, "Nothing!"

Jesus taught the same truth: "Without me ye can do nothing" (John 15:5, KJV). Fallen man, unregenerate man, is the source of all the injustice on earth. It is the nature of evil men to hate, to oppress, and to react in hostility and violence to those about them.

After we have oppressed others, we will go further to exploit them. "If thou seest the oppression of the poor, and violent perverting of judgment and justice in a province, marvel not at the matter" (5:8, KJV). First comes the oppression of the poor, then the violent perversion of judgment and justice. The word "perverting" literally means "robbery."

Unregenerate man has no basic sympathy, no concern for others (4:1). Anytime someone is kind, considerate, fair, and just, it is for his own advantage if he does not have God in his heart. Unregenerate man is a scheming creature who will manipulate and exploit those around him. This matter of oppression is so vicious that even a wise man can be turned into a monster of cruelty. "The wise man is turned into a fool by a bribe; it destroys his understanding" (7:7). Even a man who seems wise and credulous will become a monster of cruelty if he does not have God in his heart.

Ecclesiastes shows that wicked conduct causes deterioration of man's moral fiber. There is no sin that man will

The Inequities of Life

not commit, no injustice that he will not perpetrate—nothing that he will not do without God in his life. The Preacher of Ecclesiastes called those who live on such a level "fools." "Finishing is better than starting! Patience is better than pride! Don't be quick-tempered—that is being a fool" (7:8).

NO LASTING MEANING
People who take advantage of others are never happy. There is never any real meaning or purpose in life for them. What we do in the flesh (under the sun) does not bring happiness. The Preacher said that those who oppress others, those who take advantage of others, those who act unjustly will never find contentment in their actions. The oppressor is always dissatisfied. "Next I observed all the oppression and sadness throughout the earth—the tears of the oppressed, and no one helping them, while on the side of their oppressors were powerful allies" (4:1). They had all the strength but did not have the ability to enjoy it.

A Dallas man was saved after being a very prominent businessman in California. His father was a very hardworking and highly successful man in the East. After his father had given his life, driven himself to achieve everything he could achieve, he contracted cancer of the throat. This man said one of the most pitiful things he ever heard his father say, speaking through the hoarseness of a whisper, was: "I have given all of my life and worked hard so that I could buy anything I wanted to eat. Now I have enough money to buy anything I want, but I can't eat it." It was a pathetic illustration of a man who lives his life without God. Some bully their way through life, forcing their will, exploiting others. Ecclesiastes says that when a

Ecclesiastes
4:1-3

man like that achieves the goals that such inequity and oppression bring to him, he will never enjoy it, that it will never bring meaning and blessing to his life. The triumph of evil contains no element of solid worth. There is nothing there that is meaningful.

Those who oppress others have short-lived influence. "All this have I seen, and applied my heart unto every work that is done under the sun: there is a time wherein one man ruleth over another to his own hurt. And so I saw the wicked buried, who had come and gone from the place of the holy, and they were forgotten in the city where they had so done: this is also vanity" (8:9, 10, KJV). After they had given their lives to force their way on others, they died and were buried, and life moved on. They were soon forgotten.

Ultimate happiness is denied to a person who lives like that. "But though a man sins a hundred times and still lives, I know very well that those who fear God will be better off, unlike the wicked, who will not live long, good lives—their days shall pass away as quickly as shadows because they don't fear God" (8:12, 13). There are many people who have much power and money, who seem to be happy. But they only "seem" happy. We can never evaluate happiness by what is on the surface. When evil appears to triumph, be very sure that God in his sovereignty, in his authority, has decreed that a man who lives his life without God will not receive the fulfillment for which he seeks.

Problems that we face are problems only because we do not consult the eternal truth of God. Success of the wicked is only temporary. Because judgment is delayed, those who are wicked and evil, who live without God, often have a false sense of security. But God's judgment will indeed come. There is something very sad about a person who lives like this, who oppresses and forces his way through life. In life he is dissatisfied. In death he stands condemned before God.

PRINCIPLES OF DIVINE JUDGMENT
The Preacher spoke of principles of divine judgment. First, judgment is certain. "Moreover, I notice that throughout the earth justice is giving way to crime and even the police courts are corrupt. I said to myself, 'In due season God will judge everything man does, both good and bad' " (3:16). God has a time for everything meaningful in human experience. Since that is true, we can be very sure that God has a time for judgment. "Young man, it's wonderful to be young! Enjoy every minute of it! Do all you want to; take in everything, but realize that you must account to God for everything you do" (11:9). The writer concluded the book by saying, "For God will judge us for everything we do, including every hidden thing, good or bad" (12:14).

Second, the revelation of God's eternal truth is the only way to truly evaluate life. We have to place what God says alongside what seems to be. The man who succeeds is not always as successful as he thinks he is. The man who seems to be strong is not always as strong as he appears. We cannot measure happiness and meaning by what it appears to be. We must measure by the Word of God. That is why a search of the Word of God is the most significant search that any person could ever make. Every success, as well as every so-called disappointment, has to be viewed in the light of God's Word, which is our standard and pattern, our rule for faith and practice.

The world says, "If it feels good, do it." God's Word says, "You'd better see what I have to say about it before you act on the basis of how it feels." Everything that feels good is not good. Sometimes it brings harm to our lives. We must place the natural desire for success alongside the revelation of the Word of God. God's judgment will be consistent with his Word. When we stand before God in judgment, he will not judge us on how we felt or what we thought before we took a certain action. He is going to judge us on the basis of his Word.

Third, God will rectify the inequities of life. There are no lasting inequities in life because God will someday set the record straight.

Even in the light of such clear biblical teaching, something in the rebellious nature of man strikes out against everything that is reasonable and clear in the Word of God. We insist on doing things our way, forcing our way through life. But only in the end will we see the results of such rebellion.

The only way to lasting happiness is to love God and fear him. The things that man calls good, rather than satisfying him, will turn sour in his stomach and bitter in his heart. It will not be well with the wicked, but it shall be well with those who love God.

Paul wrote: "We know that all things work together for good to them that love God, to them who are the called according to his purpose" (Rom. 8:28, KJV). We live in uncertain times. Death comes to the godly and the ungodly. Since we are going to face death, we ought to face it in the power of the One who can make it to be a good experience for us, who can lead us through the valley of the shadow into the eternal light of his glory.

Everyone of us will face disappointment. Disease will fasten itself upon our bodies, or reverses will pressure us at some point. Tempers will flare. Friction will abound. Since these come to all of us, how much better to face them in the Spirit of God, who declares that it will be well for those who love the Lord!

*The Inequities
of Life*

Inequities will come and the ungodly or rebellious have no lasting comfort or satisfaction. But those who love God can face these inequities and injustices of life in his power. We shall not be beaten down by circumstances, but ride the crest of victory.

9 Someone to Care
Ecclesiastes 4:7-12

THE PREACHER next attempted to find happiness through relationships. One kind of person surrounds himself with many relationships. Another tries to be independent of any relationships. Both are attempting to find happiness. The writer will show to both types of person the futility of human companionship as a means to meet the deepest needs of their hearts.

"Then I returned, and I saw vanity under the sun. There is one alone, and there is not a second; yea, he hath neither child nor brother: yet is there no end of all his labour; neither is his eye satisfied with riches; neither saith he, For whom do I labour, and bereave my soul of good? This is also vanity, yea, it is a sore travail.

"Two are better than one; because they have a good reward for their labour. For if they fall, the one will lift up his fellow: but woe to him that is alone when he falleth; for he hath not another to help him up. Again, if two lie together, then they have heat: but how can one be warm alone? And if one prevail against him, two shall withstand him; and a threefold cord is not quickly broken" (4:7-12, KJV).

A tremendous sense of urgency exists in our hearts to belong to someone else. The Preacher spoke of that sense of loneliness that plunges us into gloom and despair.

Some people deal with this difficulty by entering into relationships, hoping to find the solution to their despair and loneliness. Others turn to isolation, to building walls, and to avoiding any kind of relationship with others. Even that is an attempt to find meaning, purpose, and happiness in life.

The first verse tells us that in the energy of the flesh, these efforts are vanity. There is no meaning in any relationship outside of God. Verse sixteen concludes by saying it is all foolishness, distress of spirit, and anxiety.

ISOLATION

In the passage above, the man who isolated himself was probably a single man, but that is not significant to the passage itself. The key is that he was rich and had withdrawn himself from everybody else so no one would make demands on him. He had plenty of the goods of this world but he had intentionally built a wall around himself. Some people refuse to let others into their hearts, to let others know them. The person who isolates himself does not have the reward of companionship. The loneliness that settled in upon his soul was brought on by his inordinate desire for wealth. He isolated himself intentionally because he was greedy, unwilling to share. Some people isolate themselves because they are proud. They don't want people to know that they hurt, so they won't reveal their vulnerability. While we cannot perhaps identify with the man isolating himself intentionally because of his wealth, we can identify with isolation.

It is obvious, when we read about this man, that it would not have made any difference if he had had a family. He would have had no time for them. He would have convinced himself that the important thing was to provide for them. He would be occupied with something

Ecclesiastes 4:7-12

he considered greater than the relationships within the home. We have the feeling that if he had had someone to whom he was responsible, he wouldn't have had the time for the person. He is a picture of lonely, pointless busyness—but with no purpose at all. The Preacher pointed out that the person who intentionally isolates himself will not find comfort but vexation of spirit.

A second kind of isolation implied in this passage is the isolation which is forced upon us. Some intentionally isolate themselves, but others, through death or separation, are forced into it. They did not choose to have a wall built around them but it happened anyway.

Certainly, the person who is forced into isolation can, with tears and grief, ask the question, "For whom do I labour and bereave my soul of good?" (4:8, KJV). No one can erect sufficient defenses for loneliness. We know how hard it is for individuals to cope when loneliness is forced upon them.

COMPANIONSHIP

The writer of Ecclesiastes tried to cope with his isolation by seeking pleasure with companions. He seemed to be trying to solve his lack of direction and purpose by surrounding himself with people. Many of us feel that if we had someone to relate to we would solve all of our problems. But when we surround ourselves with friends or companions of our own choosing, we only deepen the difficulty in which we find ourselves.

The writer of Ecclesiastes pointed out how he sought the companionship of friends for pleasure in his own strength. "Next I bought slaves, both men and women, and others were born within my household. I also bred great herds and flocks, more than any of the kings before me. I collected silver and gold as taxes from many kings and provinces. In the cultural arts, I organized men's and women's choirs and orchestras. And then there were my many beautiful concubines" (2:7, 8). He surrounded himself with people who would cater to his whims, people who would respond as he instructed them, people who would be there to provide for his needs. The conclusion was that it was all worth nothing.

Sometimes we surround ourselves with those who think like us, who will boost our ego, and cater to our whims, because we think that will provide happiness. But companionship like those mentioned brought no satisfaction to the writer's heart.

So he tried entertainment, obtaining singers and orchestras. Whatever men and women could do together in entertainment groups to boost his ego and cater to his pleasure, he tried it. And he found no pleasure, no value in it all.

One of the most common ways men try to solve their loneliness today is in the social establishments. Our society is filled with people looking for companionship, some way to solve their loneliness problem. They run in groups. They go where people are. That is why some people come to church. Church may be the best way to try to solve the loneliness problem, but it is the same motivation that takes others to bars. It is an attempt, in the energy of the flesh, to provide for the longing in the heart. We think that if we can just be with a group, and be part of things that are happening, we will find satisfaction. Unfortunately, the end is vexation of spirit and vanity. In such there is nothing worthwhile.

The Preacher wrote, "I searched everywhere, determined to find wisdom and the reason for things, and to prove to myself the wickedness of folly, and that foolishness is madness. A prostitute is more bitter than death. May it please God that you escape from her, but sinners don't evade her snares" (7:25, 26). He tried the excesses of

*Ecclesiastes
4:7-12*

immorality, sexual and sensual pleasures, to solve the emptiness in his heart. Many people today try to solve the emptiness and loneliness of their hearts that way. Sometimes it involves a special kind of companionship with someone of the opposite sex—letting down guidelines to try to please our physical and emotional appetites. The writer of Ecclesiastes did that, and he said it was foolishness, madness.

The New Testament says that whoever commits immorality sins against his own body (1 Cor. 6:18). Many of the physical ailments prevalent today are because of sexual immorality. We sin against our bodies as well as against our own emotions by indulging in such relationships. The tragedy is that they leave us guilty, ashamed, and empty. There is no meaning in it at all.

The answer is not just relating to somebody or anybody. We need *the* person God wants us to have. Whatever relationships are established need to be God-inspired as much as anything else in our lives.

PARTNERSHIP

The Preacher told how to build meaningful relationships that can bring happiness. "Two are better than one; because they have a good reward for their labour" (4:9, KJV). God wants to give us a sharing partnership. Some of us may have lost mates and we feel that we will never have another companion. But that doesn't mean that we cannot share our lives with someone else. Even without a mate, we can share in other dimensions. Marriage is only one way.

It may be that if God shuts the door to marriage, he will open the door for other kinds of sharing and companionship. We must not feel that the loneliness forced upon us is going to be permanent. It may be that God will give us new directions in our contacts with others.

The Preacher talked about the sympathy and support of such partnership. "If one falls, the other pulls him up, but if a man falls when he is alone, he's in trouble. Also, on a cold night, two under the same blanket gain warmth from each other, but how can one be warm alone?" (4:10, 11). We need the warmth, emotional and physical, that we can give to each other. For whatever reason we fall, we may need someone to pick us up, to believe in us. "If you love someone you will be loyal to him no matter what the cost. You will always believe in him, always expect the best of him, and always stand your ground in defending him" (1 Cor. 13:7). Everyone needs someone to believe in him. "A true friend is always loyal, and a brother is born to help in time of need" (Prov. 17:17). We need the encouragement of other people. We cannot give true sympathy by proxy.

One of the heaviest burdens I have as a pastor is when someone has a sickness or death in the family and doesn't tell me. I cannot share my concern by proxy, by sending someone else. There is no way I can share concern and sympathy and make it meaningful except by doing it myself. Close contact is needed to reveal the tenderness of genuine love. Such relationships bring us in touch with those who love us, who care about us, whose hearts support us sympathetically. They provide strength in the battle of life. "And one standing alone can be attacked and defeated, but two can stand back-to-back and conquer; three is even better, for a triple-braided cord is not easily broken" (4:12).

Some think the triple-braided cord refers to marriage in which the husband and wife have children. The children become the third strand of the cord. That does not seem to be consistent with the passage, however. Others feel it means that friendship has a way of breeding more friends, and when we have a partnership with one per-

Ecclesiastes 4:7-12

son, it is very easy for that partnership to multiply. If we have one friend, our sphere of influence will grow and we will soon have more than one friend.

Others think that the triple-braided cord is two people who have come together in the Lord. When they share companionship, encouragement, and support in the Lord, the Lord becomes that third strand that binds them together. It is not a quickly dissolved relationship when the Lord is the third cord that ties it together.

Everyone has struggles; everyone faces battles in life. The Preacher declared that the sweet companionship we enjoy in the Lord gives us someone who believes in us, someone who rescues us in the heat of battle. A true friend never deserts his friend. He never runs away. The pressures can't pull that relationship apart, distort, or destroy it because the partnership was established in the Lord. "There are friends who pretend to be friends, but there is a friend who sticks closer than a brother" (Prov. 18:24). This third view seems the best interpretation of the triple-braided cord.

People need people. No one can make it entirely on his own, no matter how strong he thinks he is. God brought Eve to Adam because he knew Adam couldn't make it alone. God gave husbands and wives to each other. He gave us brothers and sisters. He gave us friends and companions because no man is an island. Our hurts are not unique. We need others to soothe the wounds, to care about us, to believe in us. When God gave us the Church, he could have designed it so we could all worship independently of each other. But he knew we need to draw upon the strength of one another.

There are days when I am weak, when I am down and need encouragement. Some days you are weak and struggling and need a hand of encouragement and love extended to you. We need each other. But even companionship is empty without God, which is the essence of what Ecclesiastes says. The relationships that we desperately need can be distorted, destroyed, empty, and lacking in fulfillment if God is not in them. Whatever relationships we establish ought to be in the Lord, for without him, even companionship is vain.

We need somebody, but not just anybody. We need the companionship and friendship that God can bring into our lives. If we seek God with all our hearts and make him the pursuit of our lives, he will give us relationships that are lasting and strong, relationships of love, encouragement, meaning, and purpose.

10
Dangerous Worship
Ecclesiastes 5:1-7

WE DO MANY THINGS casually that place us in great jeopardy spiritually. Some things God will not tolerate. It would be wise for us to discover what those things are. The writer of Ecclesiastes listed some of them to which we need to give careful attention.

"Keep thy foot when thou goest to the house of God, and be more ready to hear, than to give the sacrifice of fools: for they consider not that they do evil. Be not rash with thy mouth, and let not thine heart be hasty to utter anything before God: for God is in heaven, and thou upon earth: therefore let thy words be few. For a dream cometh through the multitude of business; and a fool's voice is known by multitude of words. When thou vowest a vow unto God, defer not to pay it; for he hath no pleasure in fools: pay that which thou hast vowed. Better is it that thou shouldest not vow, than that thou shouldest vow and not pay. Suffer not thy mouth to cause thy flesh to sin; neither say thou before the angel, that it was an error: wherefore should God be angry at thy voice, and destroy the work of thine hands? For in the multitude of dreams and many words there are also divers vanities: but fear thou God" (5:1-7, KJV).

The Preacher began with a solemn warning: "Keep thy foot." Translated in our language today, it is: "Watch your step!" We are reminded that going to the house of God is a serious matter. Going in the wrong spirit is sometimes the very worst thing we can do. If we come with a wrong spirit or attitude, with a disposition that is insulting to God, we have indeed created difficulty for ourselves. The way we come into worship reveals our hearts. We must watch our steps, watch how we conduct ourselves in worship, since we are revealing our hearts by our conduct.

This passage is directed against the superficially religious, not against the inwardly devout. It is against those who are hypocritical in their worship, whose hearts are not in their actions. The Jewish people did not openly despise the Word of God. They had already discovered how God's judgment came upon them when they rebelled against his Word. These people were just the opposite. They followed the law to the letter. They went through the ritual of worship outwardly. They were in the synagogue when they were supposed to be. They bowed at the proper time; they responded outwardly in every way as God had commanded. But inwardly they were disobedient. Their worship was little more than mechanical observance. After the writer of Ecclesiastes had spent a great deal of time talking about the vanity of all the things in the world, he painted a picture for us of life under the sun. Here he said to us, in effect, "Since you are living in the midst of vanity, be very careful that you don't become vain in the one area where it is the easiest for you to be vain—in the outward ritual of your religion."

The easiest place for us to insult God and blaspheme is in the church. The easiest place to lose the meaning of worship is in the worship service, which can become perfunctory and performance-oriented. We may enter and leave a house of worship and never have worshiped at all.

PRESENCE

The writer of Ecclesiastes said four things about worship. First, we see our presence in the place of worship. "Keep thy foot when thou goest to the house of God and be more ready to hear, than to give the sacrifice of fools: for they consider not that they do evil" (5:1, KJV). When we go to the place of worship, we must be ready to hear. This means more than merely listening to the words. The Old Testament equates "hearing the Word of God" with obeying the Word of God. When we come to the house of God, we come that we may hear his Word and obey.

We cannot hear and obey the Word of God if we are not tuned in to what God is saying. It is an insult to talk during a sermon—not a slight to the preacher, but to God. The words are God's message. When we come to the house of God, the Preacher says, "Keep your ears open and your mouth shut" (5:1).

PREPARATION

We are warned here that as we go into the house of God, we are to be more ready to hear than to give "the sacrifice of fools." The word "fools" is a strong word. The "sacrifice of fools" here refers to a fool's voice. The "sacrifice" is the act of people who think they can appease God by going through the motions of religion. They come to a worship service out of custom. They come with their minds preoccupied, thinking of things other than what God has said. They have not come to hear God, but to solve the problems they are going to face at work the next day, the family difficulty, or some estranged friendship. Their minds are clouded and preoccupied with a thousand other things. That is the sacrifice of fools. God is not at all pleased at our offer to him of such a sacrifice when he instead desires a listening ear and an open heart.

The Preacher doesn't condemn all sacrifice, but rather the sacrifice of fools. He does not condemn the ritual, but the meaningless outward form. He condemns the man who thinks that by outward form he has worshiped. Fools are not aware of the evil they are doing. These are good people he is talking about, not scoundrels, nor malicious people who curse God. He is talking about people who are ignorant. They evidently don't understand that God requires in their worship the best fruit of their minds and hearts. He says they have come to worship carelessly and without understanding that their worship should involve concentration, reverence, and commitment. Rather than being scoundrels, they are simply fools.

That means there is hope for us. None of us would dare say that we do not sometimes offer the sacrifice of fools or that sometimes our minds aren't preoccupied at worship. We all come to church tired sometimes, and we are glad when the service is over. But, the Preacher said, "Watch your step." We must think about worship before we leave home. We have all caught ourselves being mentally removed from where we are. If we put words to our thoughts, we would say, "What in the world am I doing here?" Worship involves preparation. If we are to watch our steps and bring listening ears and responsive hearts to the Word of God, we ought to prepare for worship. There ought to be spiritual as well as physical preparation. We take time to make our appearance acceptable, so we ought to make the same kind of spiritual preparation. How sad when we think that God is pleased just because we have gone through the outward motion of worship! Tragically, fools do not understand that what they do is evil.

PRAYER

The Preacher spoke of our prayer lives in worship. "Don't be a fool who doesn't even realize it is sinful to make rash promises to God, for he is in heaven and you are only on earth, so let your words be few. Just as being too busy

Ecclesiastes 5:1-7

gives you nightmares, so being a fool makes you a blabbermouth" (5:2, 3). First, we ought to avoid irreverent worship, such as carrying on conversations in church when we ought to be listening or praying. "Those who are rash with their mouths" could be a reference to those who speak or pray in church. Many words don't make a person spiritual. Some of the most carnal people can pray verbally the most beautiful prayers. Some people pray beautifully, and yet they are used by Satan to split churches with their character assassinations.

We need to remember who God is. When we pray, we are talking to the eternal, infinite God in heaven. God is not a bosom buddy! One of the great heresies of our day is the manner of familiarity with which some people are encouraging others to pray. He may be the best friend we have ever had, but we are never supposed to be flippantly familiar with him. We approach him as the holy God. We must not be hasty with our hearts to utter anything before God. Our words should be few and carefully chosen.

Our prayers must seem ridiculous to God. We think we are praying when we are simply telling God facts that he already knows. It would be better for us to say a few words in reverence than to be verbose and insulting to him. Our words need to be few and we need to remember to whom we are praying. When we enter the place of worship, we need to understand that we are worshiping God who made himself visible in the person of Jesus Christ. When we come to worship, we come to worship God.

We usually think something is wrong if there is ever a moment of silence. Many think that the most beautiful sound in the world is the sound of their own voice. The writer of Ecclesiastes says, "Don't be rash with your mouth. Don't be hasty to let your heart utter something before God that is not right. Don't try to impress God." The multitude of our words reveals that we are fools.

PROMISES

"So when you talk to God and vow to him that you will do something, don't delay in doing it, for God has no pleasure in fools. Keep your promise to him. It is far better not to say you'll do something than to say you will and then not do it. In that case, your mouth is making you sin. Don't try to defend yourself by telling the messenger from God that it was all a mistake [to make the vow]. That would make God very angry; and he might destroy your prosperity" (5:4-6). When we vow to God, we are to perform it. Nowhere in the Old Testament law was man required to make a vow to God. It was not a part of the Old Testament ritual, but if the worshiper did choose to make a vow, God said, "Don't do it casually or carelessly, because if you choose to make a vow, be sure you pay it." If we choose to make a promise to God, for our sake, we had better keep it.

The Preacher said, "It is better that you should not vow than to make promises you don't keep." Moses warned: "When you make a vow to the Lord, be prompt in doing whatever it is you promised him, for the Lord demands that you promptly fulfill your vows; it is a sin if you don't. (But it is not a sin if you refrain from vowing!) Once you make the vow, you must be careful to do as you have said, for it was your choice, and you have vowed to the Lord your God" (Deut. 23:21, 22).

I wish we understood the power of words. It was a word that God spoke that created the world. The words we speak are very strong. God says that our words are so significant and important that if we speak a word of promise to him, it is imperative that we do what we said we would do. Don't make promises you can't or won't keep.

What comes out of our mouths reveals what is in our hearts. Our mouths can cause our flesh to sin. The words that we speak may often be critical or contentious, casual

Ecclesiastes 5:1-7

or careless. But the most serious misuse is an unkept promise to God.

In the Old Testament, if a person sinned through weakness, a sacrifice was to be made to provide atonement for that sin. But if the individual sinned presumptuously, willfully, there was no sacrifice in the Jewish system for such a sin.

We find the same language in the New Testament: "For if we sin wilfully after that we have received the knowledge of the truth, there remaineth no more sacrifice for sins" (Heb. 10:26, KJV). It is a fearful thing for us to play games with God in worship. There is a great difference between sins of weakness and deliberate sins. The Preacher of Ecclesiastes warned us that if we don't worship as we ought, if we willfully mock God, judgment is going to come upon us.

The Preacher explained: "That would make God very angry." Someone may come to church, sing in the choir, lift his voice in praise to God, and yet God may be angry with all of it. We may voice a prayer, but when it comes to the ear of God, he may be angry with it. By the careless, casual way we come to worship, we expose ourselves to divine anger. Such conduct will result in the total loss of anything worthwhile in our worship efforts.

It frightens me to see people take such a casual approach to prayer or worship, because God says when we approach him casually, we are exposing ourselves to his anger. No amount of emphasis on God's grace can justify our taking liberties with him. We can talk about grace all we want to, but it does not give us license to make light of God or to be casual with him.

The book of Ecclesiastes has described throughout a world of vanity: popularity, wealth, earthly prestige—all of the things we strive to get. These things are all vain if done in the flesh. Next the writer describes a situation in which God's people come mechanically, methodically, and faithfully into the house of worship, and this, too, is vanity. "Dreaming instead of doing is foolishness, and there is ruin in a flood of empty words; fear God instead" (5:7). Not only is it vanity, but it provokes the anger of God.

The only way to avoid dangerous worship is to have a deep sense of awe and respect for God. We have made God to be the Man Upstairs, the Benevolent Grandfather, the Man Next Door, our Bosom Buddy, our Friend. While he may be all of those, he is God. We approach him as God. Better not come at all than to mock his presence. It is better not to attend at all than to go through the motions in a way that calls for his anger to fall upon us.

11 The Peril of Wealth
Ecclesiastes 5:10-17

BIBLICAL REFERENCES to the rich man do not always refer to people with a lot of money. Many times the reference is to a person who lives for wealth and material possessions. A poor man might also fit that category. The belief that what really matters is wealth that can be amassed during a lifetime could be called the peril of wealth. Those who are rich do have great influence and power in our society.

Material possessions have a way of elevating people in the eyes of the community. But while there are some advantages to affluence, there are also some great dangers. In Ecclesiastes, the writer has already talked about the poor who were oppressed and in great sorrow because they were stripped of material possessions. He turns next to those who are concerned because they don't think they have enough yet. The Preacher warns them that being rich is not what it appears to be.

AN INSATIABLE HUNGER FOR MORE

The first peril that comes to someone who lives for possessions is the insatiable hunger for more that accompanies it. "He who loves money shall never have enough" (5:10).

The Peril of Wealth

We would think those who had something would be happy when they get more, but the opposite is true. Wealth creates the desire for more. The human heart in its natural environment, apart from God, is always that way. Why did the rich man, in the parable Nathan told David, steal the lamb from the poor man to feed his guests? He didn't have to, or need to do so. In the heart of those who live for possessions is an insatiable hunger for more. Our possessions simply stimulate the desire for more. And when we get more, it feeds the desire that is never satisfied.

This hunger extends to everything material—sex, drugs, popularity, possessions, whatever the world can give us. Little things progress to great things. The man who flirts with small temptations will become a slave to great sins.

If there is anything worse than the addiction to money and material things, it is the heartache and emptiness that these things leave.

It does not matter whether we are struggling to pay the bills and desiring more or whether we have money in the bank. If we live for that which the world can give to us physically, we are only feeding a habit for which there is no satisfaction. But the man with eternity in his heart needs more satisfying nourishment than this world can provide. He does not live for this world.

AN INCREASED UPKEEP

Those who live for material things find that their upkeep costs are heavy. "The more you have, the more you spend, right up to the limits of your income, so what is the advantage of wealth—except perhaps to watch it as it runs through your fingers!" (5:11). When a person has the things of this world, a swarm of people gravitate toward

Ecclesiastes
5:10-17

him who increase his upkeep. His attendants, hangers-on who swarm around him, only increase his cares and eat up his profit. A complex establishment grows up around affluence.

Isaiah spoke of this problem in a most humorous way: "I will make of him a strong and steady peg to support my people; they will load him with responsibility and he will be an honor to his family name. But the Lord will pull out that other peg that seems to be so firmly fastened to the wall! It will come out and fall to the ground, and everything it supports will fall with it, for the Lord has spoken" (Isa. 22:23-25). You have seen pegs for hanging coats, or perhaps a hall tree or hatrack. Every time someone comes by he puts something else on it until finally it breaks and falls on the floor. That is the picture.

A wealthy, prestigious man is like a peg on the wall. All the people swarm by and latch onto him. Finally, the peg comes down and everything with it. That is part of the peril of being wealthy. Too many people hang onto you.

The rich are always subject to claims proportionate to their wealth. There is always tremendous pressure from people who will hang unto the wealth of other people. That is not to disparage those very legitimate enterprises which have a claim on the wealthy. But when we have the things this world gives, we may not be prepared for the complexity that comes with it.

AN INEVITABLE DISCOMFORT
Wealth also brings inevitable discomfort. "The man who works hard sleeps well, whether he eats little or much, but the rich must worry and suffer insomnia. There is another serious problem I have seen everywhere—savings are put into risky investments that turn sour, and soon there is nothing left to pass on to one's son" (5:12-14). Wealth is

The Peril of Wealth

only a handful that slips through the fingers of the one who lives for things. The poor rest well, but the person who lives for material things will have a hard time sleeping (5:12).

The rich often cannot sleep because they eat too much! All the spas, saunas, and exercise studios, and all the jogging take a great deal of time and money as we attempt to solve the problems that indulgence creates. In our affluence, we have created a problem which we have to develop an entire new industry to solve. The rich cannot get their money-making projects out of their minds. They are constantly overcome.

When he was cast out of the garden, Adam's curse had one bright mercy spot. "In the sweat of thy face shalt thou eat bread" (Gen. 3:19, KJV). One of the blessings of work, which the rich don't appreciate, will be that the worker enjoys his food and digests it well.

The man who is pursuing the things of this world is after all the things he can get. But God declares to us that it is never good to make temporal things the sole purpose of life. "There is a sore evil which I have seen under the sun, namely riches kept for the owners thereof to their hurt" (5:13, KJV). Man may see wealth as good, but God says that it is evil to live for it. God never intended for us to be possessed by our possessions. We best possess our possessions when we put them at God's disposal, and let them come under his authority. We must hold things in our hands and not let them worm their way into our hearts.

God reveals to us in his Word that it is not ten percent of our possessions that belong to him but one hundred percent. If we try to give him a tenth and hoard the nine-tenths, or try to keep it all, we will do it to our own harm. The person who lives for things will never know the joy of the Lord because his channel is too narrow, his scope is too small, his reach is too short. Man was never intended to be so possessed by his wealth that he would not release

*Ecclesiastes
5:10-17*

it. Whatever we possess is the Lord's, and if we want happiness, we must release it to him.

The Apostle Paul made an appeal for an offering for the saints in Jerusalem. He used the Macedonian Christians as an example by saying that they first gave themselves unto the Lord. "They begged us to take an offering. Out of their deep poverty, they gave." And God gave them great joy. Their happiness came because they released that which God had entrusted to them and God used it to bless others.

The Preacher talked about business losses (5:14). A crash in the man's business took away his riches and he had nothing to leave his heir. That man who lived only for this world, whether he had his possessions at his death or not, left nothing of lasting value to his heirs. If all a person leaves to those who come after him is a pile of material possessions, he is poor indeed. There are far greater things to leave our heirs than that, such as the greatness of a godly life, the discipline of a committed spirit to God, and the witness of consistent Christianity lived out before them. That is the heritage that we should leave. If we leave them everything else and don't leave them that, we have left nothing of any lasting value.

People can make all the money they want, and amass all the material possessions they can, but they will not take one penny with them. All the hard work and all the ulcers they get trying to make it, all the effort and energy they give to protecting it, are wasted, for when they die, someone else gets it. The government will get some of it, which is enough to make us want to be poor.

The Preacher mentioned this vanity: "I also observed another piece of foolishness around the earth. This is the case of a man who is quite alone, without a son or brother, yet he works hard to keep gaining more riches, and to whom will he leave it all? And why is he giving up so much now? It is all so pointless and depressing" (4:7, 8).

*The Peril
of Wealth*

The labors of man without God have no solid and lasting value. Who would want his tombstone epitaph to read: "He labored to the wind" (5:16, KJV)? What a tragedy for someone to labor and leave nothing of lasting value. "All the rest of his life he is under a cloud—gloomy, discouraged, frustrated, and angry." Such a person passes his life in sadness with no power to enjoy what he has. Increasing infirmities produce more misery, and he is more unhappy than ever.

Whatever we gain materially, we do so because God lets us. We hear a lot about self-made men, about people whose genius created empires. But that is only because the sovereign God lets them do so. God may allow them to amass the fortune, but he may not allow them to enjoy it.

A hunger in the heart for God is never appeased by anything else. When we choose rather to give ourselves to that which is temporal, we find that we gain no satisfaction from it. Think, for example, of something you may have wanted five years ago, something that you thought would really make you happy if you had it—a new car, a new position, a new piece of furniture, perhaps to get married. Apart from God, and that is where some of us live, when you got it, what happened? If you are like me, you probably wanted something else besides. You weren't as happy as you thought you would be.

One of Satan's greatest ploys is to operate in our feelings. We look at new Christians who are beaming—with big smiles and sparkling eyes. Then we imagine we know how they feel, and imagine a certain physical thrill that ought to accompany such a spiritual experience. But when we make the commitment, and we don't feel what we think we ought to feel, there is emptiness and unhappiness. Nothing based on material sensation of human life will ever bring satisfaction. If we wait to tingle like someone else tingled to get saved, we will never get saved. The Bible did not say a word about a physical feeling that was

*Ecclesiastes
5:10-17*

to accompany salvation. Nothing in the material world, nothing under the sun, should govern the conduct and decisions of godly people.

God sends discomfort to those who live for this world. Jesus said, "Seek ye first the kingdom of God, and his righteousness: and all these things shall be added unto you" (Matt. 6:33, KJV). And, "Ye cannot serve God and mammon" (Matt. 6:24, KJV).

We must choose which will be our master. We must not be mastered by that which produces only emptiness and frustration. We must be mastered by him who alone can bring meaning and purpose into our lives.

The Frivolous Spirit
Ecclesiastes 7:1-6

12

ONE OF THE GREATEST THREATS to Christian character is the temptation to a "frivolous spirit." Two passages in the book of Ecclesiastes describe this spirit.

"I said to myself, 'Come now, be merry; enjoy yourself to the full.' But I found that this, too, was futile. For it is silly to be laughing all the time; what good does it do?" (2:1, 2).

"A good name is better than precious ointment; and the day of death than the day of one's birth. It is better to go to the house of mourning, than to go to the house of feasting: for that is the end of all men; and the living will lay it to his heart. Sorrow is better than laughter; for by the sadness of the countenance the heart is made better. The heart of fools is in the house of mirth. It is better to hear the rebuke of the wise, than for a man to hear the song of fools. For as the crackling of thorns under a pot, so is the laughter of the fool: this also is vanity" (7:1-6, KJV).

The Preacher, remember, using the world's knowledge and perspectives, was talking about the way the world feasts and mourns. He was saying that the end of all men is to be sorrow and mourning.

Up to this point, the Preacher of Ecclesiastes had been honestly experimenting, seeking to use the things of the world in the very best way possible. He was not a profligate or a prodigal. He was not spurning the good things of wisdom, knowledge, or rightful pleasure. He did the very best one could do. He discussed the use of wine, yet he didn't become a drunkard. He used wisdom in the same careful way. Even using things in a good way is vanity, he said. If we will hear what he said about all these things, it will save us much heartache.

After he had tried pleasure and knowledge and all the things connected with them, he tried what we will call frivolity or mirth. It is spoken of, in this context, as laughter and feasting. The Preacher found that the frivolous approach to life was vanity also.

He was not condemning cheerfulness or saying that we should not smile or laugh. He was not speaking about a merry heart. Becoming a Christian does not destroy happiness for us. He was speaking of seeking happiness in carnal mirth, in a carnal spirit of frivolity.

It was the spirit of the man in Luke chapter twelve who became so wealthy, and after trying all the excesses of the world, found he was still not happy. So he decided to tear down his barns and build bigger ones and plant more crops. And he said to his soul: "Friend, you have enough stored away for years to come. Now take it easy! Wine, women, and song for you!" (Luke 12:19). That is the spirit the Preacher was speaking of—the loose, careless spirit of seeking happiness.

ITS DESCRIPTION

Four things are mentioned about the frivolous spirit in Ecclesiastes. First, notice the description of it. It is not necessarily doing anything immoral or criminal, for laughter and mirth are not bad in themselves. These words refer to things we might do to entertain ourselves or to pass the time, which are not in themselves wrong. But they be-

The Frivolous Spirit

come wrong when they are the primary focus of our search for happiness. Such entertainment could be a ball game or some other kind of sporting event. It could be music, leisure, a hobby of some kind—whatever we find to give us pleasure.

So the frivolous spirit is one that is preoccupied and driven by harmless amusements and entertainment, seeking things that "make us feel good," and things that feed our egos. It could be nothing more than an experience that feels good to our bodies, such as a whirlpool bath or a sauna.

One way that people have sought amusement has been through music. Many people seem to be "hooked" on it and they try to draw happiness from it. There is nothing wrong with music, but we can't really draw lasting satisfaction from anything in the world.

The frivolous spirit is pleased with what glitters and excited. Harmless amusements, sensual pleasures, laughter, song—these are the things the Preacher was talking about.

Many of us will show more concern over the outcome of the Superbowl than over our sins or the lost condition of our next-door neighbor. Such an attitude is absolutely wrong. Many of us are so preoccupied with frivolous, non-essential things that we have sought to satisfy our hearts in them. We surround ourselves with an abundance of food, with things for us to look nice in, things to enjoy and make us feel good. It is wrong when we live only for the things that feed our sensual selves.

THE DISTRESS OF A FRIVOLOUS SPIRIT

The thoughts of the man who has a frivolous spirit are scattered over a thousand hillsides. He never concentrates, or is ever able to be alone with himself. He never

*Ecclesiastes
7:1-6*

takes inventory of his life, nor is honest with himself, because his distracted mind flits here and there. His thoughts are chasing a thousand rainbows and a thousand illusive dreams that never find reality. His mind is filled with silly, trifling ideas. Everything is humorous, synthetic, unreal to him. A kind of moral insanity sets in when a heart is constantly under the wild excitement of pleasure. His is not the world where people hurt and need help, love, and encouragement. His is not the world where people find fulfillment and discover themselves. His world is controlled by uncontrollable impulses and passions.

THE DESTINY OF A FRIVOLOUS SPIRIT
The frivolous spirit has no lasting value. For example, who will remember, ten years from now, and what will it matter, who wins the Superbowl this year? There is no permanent consolation in these nonessentials. "I have tried this and I found that it is mad. I found that it has nothing good," the writer said. "What does it do? How does it help me? I tried mirth—what good came out of it? What blessing came to my life? What lasting encouragement came to me? All of these things I felt were so significant and just had to have them—what good are they now?" The frivolous heart is destined to frustration, to disgust, and weariness. That is what he meant when he said, "That is the end of all men" (7:2, KJV). The frivolous heart will one day become the very serious heart. The man who flits through life and never settles down to reality and essentials is one who, someday, at the end of life, has to deal with those very things. Disgust and weariness are the destiny of the frivolous heart.

"It is like the crackling of thorns under a pot" (7:6, KJV). This verse describes kindling wood, dry thorn bushes used to start a fire. We start fires with paper today, but we

The Frivolous Spirit

would never build a lasting fire out of it. Living for frivolous things is like trying to build a fire out of thorn bushes or paper. They crackle and pop, but don't give off lasting heat and are consumed very quickly. If we are more concerned about nonessential, frivolous things than we are about the things that really matter in life, our destiny is also a lot of noise with no permanent result.

THE DEFEAT OF A FRIVOLOUS SPIRIT
When Americans travel to other countries, they find how blessed they are. Someone said the two biggest problems Americans have are how to get a bigger garbage can and a place to park their cars. Many of the world's people literally live from one day to the next under the threat of starvation or the ravages of war.

But we have another kind of problem created by our opulence. For example, we are pushing for a four-day work week, when one of the worst things that ever happened to this country was the end of the six-day work week. We will have even more trouble with leisure time as we work less and less. Also, we are surrounded with material things that involve more and more of our attention. The garbage we dispose of is more than most of the world's people have to eat. With so many more of the frivolous things, how are we to avoid a frivolous spirit?

We must face the painful facts of life rather than avoid them by engaging in frivolous things—laughter, diversions, entertainment (7:2). How long has it been since we faced the truth about the kind of persons we are? Our hearts dwell upon every evil known to man. In all of our hearts there are lusts that could consummate in acts of disobedience and rebellion against God. That is reason enough to realize the seriousness of life.

How long has it been since we mourned for our sins?

*Ecclesiastes
7:1-6*

"Blessed are they that mourn for they shall be comforted" (Matt. 5:4, KJV). One way we defeat a frivolous spirit is by mourning over our sins. As we look at ourselves and our sins, we see our need to ask God to free us from that which is against him. Even though we keep on sinning, we tend to forget what we did yesterday. But we are reminded that we haven't arrived yet. The Apostle Paul said, "No, dear brothers, I am still not all I should be but I am bringing all my energies to bear on this one thing: Forgetting the past and looking forward to what lies ahead, I strain to reach the end of the race and receive the prize for which God is calling us up to heaven because of what Christ Jesus did for us" (Phil. 3:13, 14).

As we look ahead, we need to be reminded of ourselves. Every time we look in the mirror, we see the persons that we are. Every time we open the Word of God, we see hearts that contain every evil thought and the potential for every evil deed known to man.

But the frivolous person doesn't stop long enough to do that. The word "worship" comes from a root word that means "to stop doing what you are doing." The reason most of us can never really worship is that we cannot stop what we are doing long enough. Even in our formal worship, our minds are often so preoccupied with what we are doing that we never really stop to think about God.

To defeat a frivolous spirit, we must face the truth about ourselves. We must look at ourselves and let God cause a godly mourning over our sins to come into our hearts. We must look at the lost about us and see those who are without Jesus Christ and see that they are destined to an eternal hell. We must think about all the times we have missed the opportunities to share Christ with them, remembering that God has said we are accountable if they die in their sins because we failed to warn them (Ezek. 33:7, 8). This truth is a strong antidote to a frivolous spirit.

Perhaps if we thought of Calvary and the Savior hang-

The Frivolous Spirit

ing on the cross and could see the agony and anguish borne in his soul, it would help us defeat the frivolous spirit. Mourning for our sins is the only way to find eternal joy. The mouth of the righteous will be filled with laughter when the tears of this earthly pilgrimage have dried up. Our laughter then won't be like the crackling of thorns, but as the singing together of the morning stars, as the shouting for joy of all the sons of God.

We will never be happy as long as our happiness is dependent on how well the Dallas Cowboys play, how many cars we have to drive, or how many country clubs we belong to.

The average American spends thirty-five hours a week in front of the television set. So determined are we to be entertained, not to think about life, that we will find anything to distract us from that so we can be happy. It won't work. Someday, God will make us look at ourselves as we really are. Our emphasis should be on essential things so that we use the frivolous things as needed recreations, but not as essential to our happiness. We should decide that we will no longer determine our satisfaction in life by the things we have, but rather by the things we give in the important pursuits of life. "A good reputation is more valuable than the most expensive perfume. The day one dies is better than the day he is born!" (7:1). How can it be that the day one dies is better than one's birthday? Because if we go to the house of mourning now, when we come to death, we will be in the house of laughter and joy. But if we go to the house of laughter and diversion now, when we come to death, we will go to the house of mourning. To those who would defeat the frivolous spirit, the day of death becomes a victory day because they have not allowed nonessentials to conquer and control their lives.

The enemy of the best is not the bad but the good. We are more likely to fall for good things than for bad things. We are more likely to neglect God's call for our lives because we are too busy doing good things—not because we are doing bad things.

If there is anything that appeals to our senses controlling us, then God isn't in charge. We must let God show us what it is in our lives that is most important. What we consider most important is what we think about the most, what we love the most, what we spend the most time doing, where we put the most of our money. We must determine what is most important to us, and if it is anything less than eternal values, we must commit it to God.

Obedience in Adversity
Ecclesiastes 11:1-6

"CAST THY BREAD upon the waters: for thou shalt find it after many days. Give a portion to seven, and also to eight; for thou knowest not what evil shall be upon the earth. If the clouds be full of rain, they empty themselves upon the earth: and if the tree fall toward the south, or toward the north, in the place where the tree falleth, there it shall be. He that observeth the wind shall not sow; and he that regardeth the clouds shall not reap. As thou knowest not what is the way of the spirit, nor how the bones do grow in the womb of her that is with child: even so thou knowest not the works of God who maketh all. In the morning sow thy seed, and in the evening withhold not thine hand: for thou knowest not whether shall prosper, either this or that, or whether they both shall be alike good" (11:1-6, KJV).

"He that observeth the wind shall not sow; and he that regardeth the clouds shall not reap," the Preacher said (11:4). There is a lesson here for us. If we wait until ideal circumstances arrive before we enter upon any activity, we will not likely ever do very much. If we have a philosophy that depends on perfect conditions, we will be often frustrated, because the circumstances of life are seldom, if ever, ideal. Every labor, every enterprise, every activity, every program, every goal that we might dream to achieve, is filled with difficulty. If we are trying to start a new business and we wait to begin our venture until all the

Ecclesiastes 11:1-6

conditions are right, it will be too late and we won't begin at all. If we are investing in the stock market, and wait until the conditions are ideal, an investment will never be made. While we are hesitant, someone else is stepping out in less than ideal conditions and making a good return on his investment.

The same is true in marriage. If we wait until the ideal time we never will marry. Just before we were married, my wife sent me this poem:

The groom white of hair
Is stooped o'er his cane.
His footsteps uncertain, need guiding.
While down the church aisle,
In a wan toothless smile
The bride in a wheelchair comes riding.
Now who is this elderly couple just wed?
You will find when you've carefully explored it,
That this is that rare, most conservative pair,
Who waited until they could afford it.

Since earthly pursuits are filled with such difficulty and danger, we shouldn't think that our service to God is not also filled with difficulty and sometimes danger. We shouldn't think that the dreams God places in our hearts to do for him will be any different. Certainly those who would build the kingdom of God through his power in their lives are going to have to be bold and will have to sow and reap when it seems that there is an ill wind blowing and the clouds are ominously near. It is not likely that we would ever enter any heavenly calling if we looked only at the circumstances. We would look into our hearts, see how hostile and bitter we are, and, knowing the failures we have been in the past, feel that we could never even be saved, much less serve. God sent his Son, Jesus Christ, who came into the world as a testimony to the grace and love of God, who reaches over and above our sin to draw us to him.

The same thing is true of our Christian walk. Our lives could become threatened by conditions and feelings. People have told me they don't pray because they no longer feel like praying. If we waited until we felt like it, we would very seldom pray. The truth is that when we feel least like praying is the time we need to pray the most. We need to move beyond feelings and circumstances. We need to sow even though the time doesn't seem right and reap even though it doesn't seem a profitable time.

It is in being faithful at times when it seems most difficult that we find the best answers to prayer. Even though we feel it is like throwing pious phrases in the air, even though we feel God doesn't hear, we need to pray, because we know that he does hear.

The same is true of Bible reading. If we only do it when we think we have time, we never will. If we looked only at the circumstances, we would never witness, either. We look around us and see such wickedness and hostility toward the things of God and we become afraid to tell people about Jesus. Witnessing isn't done like that.

This is also true of giving. If we only gave in the light of human understanding and reason, we would never give very much. If we waited until we could add it all up and see our way to the end, we would never give anything. It should be enough that God says to sow, even though the wind blows ill, and reap, even though the clouds seem near.

A DANGEROUS RESPONSE

It is dangerous for us to refuse to sow when God says sow. It is dangerous for us to refuse to reap when God says reap.

Ecclesiastes 11:1-6

Whatever God tells us to do, we do it or we are being rebellious and disobedient. "Wicked" is a strong word in the Bible. One of the few times Jesus used the word was to describe the servant who hid his talent and did nothing with what God had given to him. In essence, Jesus said the most wicked man in the story was the one who did nothing. When we refuse to do what God tells us to do because the circumstances and conditions don't seem right to us, we are acting as if God doesn't know what is going on. We refuse not only to obey him but we in so doing refuse to believe him. The Apostle Paul wrote that whatever is not of faith is sin (Rom. 14:23). That kind of disobedience is a dangerous response.

Sometimes our disobedience is because of sheer laziness. We just don't want to sow or reap. The writer of Proverbs talked about the sluggard, the lazy person: "But you—all you do is sleep. When will you wake up? 'Let me sleep a little longer!' Sure, just a little more" (Prov. 6:9, 10).

"The lazy man won't go out and work. 'There might be a lion outside!' he says. He sticks to his bed like a door to its hinges! He is too tired even to lift his food from his dish to his mouth!" (Prov. 26:13-15). If a person doesn't want to serve God—if a person is lazy, it is amazing how many reasons he can find not to obey.

The Apostle Paul was once presented before the governor of one of the districts he was passing through. After Gallio listened to the arguments against Paul, the writer said very simply of him, "Gallio cared for none of these things" (Acts 18:17). He had no interest or concern for them. When it comes to witnessing, to serving God, to doing what God has placed the Church here to do, for many church people we can say, "They cared for none of these things." We can always find reasons why we don't do what God calls us to do.

Obedience in Adversity

A DARING ACTION

The Preacher called for some unusual, but daring and creative action. "Cast thy bread upon the waters: for thou shalt find it after many days. Give a portion to seven, and also to eight; for thou knowest not what evil shall be upon the earth" (11:1, 2, KJV). It seems strange to cast bread on the water. It would seem to be better to put it on the table. But he said to cast it on the water. There is no place for business as usual among God's people. We are to enter into a responsibility that leads us to the ends of the earth. Though it doesn't seem to make sense at the time, we are to move out as he commands. Daring action is called for.

That is the same kind of thing that Jesus required of the disciples the night they had been fishing without catching anything. The Lord told them to go out again and let down their nets for a draft of fish (Luke 5). They immediately began to object. "He doesn't understand. He isn't a fisherman," they probably thought. "When one fishes all night and doesn't catch anything, there is certainly no use in fishing in the morning. Fish don't bite in the morning." Simon Peter began to tell Jesus all that, but he thought better of it, so they went back out and let down their nets. They got such a catch of fish that their nets began to break. It was an unusual thing Jesus was asking them to do. It was a daring thing, and the victory came when the disciples believed him and trusted him.

Luke gave a beautiful principle for the stewardship of our possessions. "For if you give, you will get! Your gift will return to you in full and overflowing measure, pressed down, shaken together to make room for more, and running over. Whatever measure you use to give—large or small—will be used to measure what is given back to you" (Luke 6:38).

Most people feel they need to hoard all their money and save it to get rich. Jesus said, "Give and you will get!" That is daring action.

Ecclesiastes 11:1-6

A DISTINCT PURPOSE

God demonstrates that he has a distinct purpose for what he does. "If the clouds be full of rain, they empty themselves upon the earth: and if the tree fall toward the south, or toward the north, in the place where the tree falleth, there it shall be" (11:3, KJV). Clouds get full of water for one reason: to empty themselves. Clouds don't get black just so artists can paint pictures. They do it so God can accomplish his plan of watering the earth, as part of the cycle of life that God gives. Sunshine all the time in one place makes a desert. Rain all the time in one place would create havoc. God in his gracious provision for us has designed sunshine and rain, and both are part of his purpose and plan. It is God's way of reminding us that whatever he has entrusted to us of talent, time, and possession, it is given with great purpose. We have what we have in order to give it back.

Jesus declared that if we selfishly try to save our lives, we will lose them. But if we lose our lives for his sake, we find them (Matt. 16:25). The only thing we keep in our relationship with God is what we give away. If we selfishly keep for ourselves, we will deprive ourselves of that which we need to receive. If we need sympathy, then we must be sympathetic. If we need love, we need to be loving to others. We get in measure to what we give.

A DETERMINED FAITH

We need the kind of determined faith that doesn't ask God to explain everything to us before we obey him. God wants us to trust him even though we don't always understand. If we always wait for understanding, we will never take action for God. It is enough that God says, "Do it!"

When I was in the ministry some years ago, I received a call to pastor a church in another state. I wrote my dad and asked his advice on how to make the decision whether to go or not. I received a special delivery letter from him, telling me all the things I needed to consider in making a good decision. Then in the last sentence he told me that when I had done all these things, to push them aside, get on my knees, and ask the Lord what he wanted me to do. That was the ultimate test. What does God want—not what does my understanding tell me to do.

As Christians we know there are many things we should do, though we may not understand why. If we waited until we did understand, we would never do what God has called us to do.

A DELIBERATE DILIGENCE
The Preacher said we needed a deliberate diligence in our lives. "In the morning sow thy seed, and in the evening withhold not thine hand: for thou knowest not whether shall prosper, either this or that, or whether they both shall be alike good" (11:6, KJV). We must do what we know God wants us to do and keep at it. Don't be weary in well doing. Obey God. Follow him with diligence. We say we don't know whether God wants us to go to Brazil or Africa, whether he wants us to teach or preach. But we know whether our attitude toward our fellow Christian, toward our church, or toward our job is what God wants it to be. What God wants is for us to start where we are and do something about our life.

If we are not careful, we will spend our lifetime trying to settle whether the United States should have diplomatic relations with Red China or Taiwan and never determine whether *we* are going to have diplomatic relations with the Holy Spirit of God. We will spend our time trying to answer questions over which we have no control. It may make no difference what we think about international

Ecclesiastes 11:1-6

politics. But what does make a difference is what we think about Jesus Christ. That is something we have control over and should do something about. "Early in the morning sow your seed, in the evening don't withhold your hand" (11:6, KJV). The opportunity God has given to us is an opportunity we need to grasp and utilize for his glory and for his purpose.

14

Coming Judgment
Ecclesiastes 11:9, 10

"REJOICE, O YOUNG MAN, in thy youth; and let thy heart cheer thee in the days of thy youth, and walk in the ways of thine heart, and in the sight of thine eyes: but know thou, that for all these things, God will bring thee into judgment. Therefore remove sorrow from thy heart, and put away evil from thy flesh: for childhood and youth are vanity" (11:9, 10).

This brief passage is one of the most interesting studies of judgment found in Scripture. It is a truth often missing in other more sternly worded messages of judgment because it offers a positive and hopeful note. The writer of Ecclesiastes, in dealing with judgment, wanted to offer hope. Up until this time, he has dealt with things as they are "under the sun," apart from God. But here, as he talked about judgment, he focused on God and our relationship to him. He painted a glimmer of hope and anticipation in what God will do for us even in judgment.

APPREHENSION

Three basic thoughts in these verses relate to judgment. The first one is apprehension, which sounds as though we are nervous because of something about to happen. But the meaning here is apprehending, or taking hold of something. The key is in the ninth verse in the phrase "know thou," which means to have apprehended knowledge in such a way that it controls our lives. If we know that God is going to bring judgment, such knowledge should affect us—knowledge that *we* have apprehended, which in turn has apprehended *us* and changed our lives.

Many know the truth but do not live by it. Christians who are not faithful with their witness, their possessions, their time and talents have the intellectual knowledge of how they ought to live. But knowing has not changed their lives. The truth of God which the Preacher wrote about was the kind that had secured the hearers' minds —apprehended them so that they will never be the same.

The Preacher's mention of "rejoicing in your youth" was not being negative. He was not suggesting that if a young person enjoys being young that he is sinning. Rather, he was suggesting that every young man should view the pleasures and enjoyments of life in the light of the approaching judgment. The doctrine of judgment was meant to influence us. We are to enjoy life and the things of life in such a way that enjoyment is regulated by the prospects of judgment.

There are judgments of God along the way. There is the judgment of a stricken conscience, the judgment of the chastening hand of God upon us. But he meant the final judgment when he said, "God will bring you into judgment." The original language has a definite article: "God will bring you into *the* judgment."

The New Testament concept is that if we are saved, people should notice the difference. "Therefore if any man be in Christ, he is a new creature: old things are passed away; behold, all things are become new" (2 Cor. 5:17, KJV). When this truth has taken hold of our lives, such knowledge will not let us continue to be mediocre, carnal, and sinful. Perhaps the church has done a great injustice by not emphasizing this kind of judgment more. A true knowledge of judgment would brighten the whole horizon of life.

ACCOUNTABILITY
The fact of judgment indicates accountability. Unless someone were accountable, there would be no such thing as judgment. Human responsibility makes future judgment imperative. Judgment would be meaningless if man were not responsible. If a man is accountable, if man is responsible, then future judgment is an absolute essential.

The truths of God do not always accommodate themselves to human logic. We could explain hell with logic because of man's attitude, his evil nature, his viciousness. In looking at our world today, we find prisons for those who cannot be contributing citizens of society, and policemen who have to enforce the laws. Everywhere we turn there is evidence of enforcement of law or punishment for law breaking. That is something we can see and understand because we are considered responsible citizens of our society. The same kind of responsibility and accountability exists between people and God. We are not responsible and accountable for what we don't have but we are accountable for what God has placed in our hands —the opportunities, our talents, our possessions, the time alloted to us. The whole idea of judgment speaks of accountability.

Accountability is not entirely a negative concept. The fact that we are accountable makes us face the possibility that we may, through his grace, obtain the reward of the righteous. That is the essence of the story of the talents in Matthew 25:12-30. One man received a certain number of talents, another less, and still another man only one. The two who had the most talents received a reward, a wel-

*Ecclesiastes
11:9, 10*

come home from the Master because they had been faithful. Theirs was a good judgment. But the man who had dissipated his truth by not using what was given to him was found guilty. Accountability does not just mean that we may be condemned. It could mean that we will receive reward.

This idea of judgment has several important points. First, since God cares enough to judge everything, then nothing in our lives can be pointless or insignificant. Since God is going to bring every secret thing to light, every little thing to judgment, that ought to teach us that everything about our lives is significant.

That God is interested in every area of our lives—every problem, every relationship—is good news. Nothing is too small to talk to God about, nothing too insignificant.

My daughter called me one morning and said, "Daddy, I have lost my contact lens in the carpet. Would you pray that I would find it?" I told her I would, and she hung up. I prayed, and about sixty seconds later, the phone rang. It was Terri. She had found it. She seemed surprised, but I wasn't, for I knew God was concerned about everything—even something as tiny as a contact lens. Everything is important because he is going to bring everything into judgment. That truth broadens the whole horizon of life. It means that we never engage in insignificant things. Understanding that truth will help us comprehend how God relates to every area of life.

It is good news that God takes the things we call little and insignificant into his care and concern. There is a good reason for that. Big rocks are seldom made out of little rocks. Usually it is through the compacting of particles of fine sand that the big rocks are made. In the same way, big problems are not made out of little problems. They are usually made out of seemingly insignificant things that we didn't think mattered until they came together to build a mountain of opposition to our happiness and success.

A minister I knew in my youth had a unique way of talking about sin. He brought a spool of thread and had us wrap one strand around his wrists. He then asked, "Do you think I can break that?" Of course he could, and he did. Then we doubled the thread around his wrists. He broke that, so we doubled the strands again. We continued adding strand after strand until the accumulation of threads formed a strong little cord that he could not break. Yet it was made up of tiny little threads, each of which he could break separately. Sin is like that, he explained to us.

It is in the little areas of life where we fail God. Little failures cause us to fail him in large areas. We don't think we would ever do anything that would be considered a great sin. We might not today. But if we are negligent in the little areas, if we neglect to pray, to worship, to be obedient to him in the everyday affairs of life, these things will become the threads that double, and double again and again until they bind us and we end up doing those things we thought we would never do. It all started with something we thought was unimportant.

"For God shall bring every work into judgment, with every secret thing, whether it be good, or whether it be evil" (12:14, KJV). God will judge the things no one else can see, such as our attitudes. We see only the outside of people and things. In this judgment, God is going to bring to light those things which are impossible to judge by human standards. The true heart attitude as we go through the motions of religion will be judged. We are accountable not only for what we do but for why we do it. Accountability is part of this judgment.

APPROVAL

Judgment does not necessarily mean condemnation. He who lives in an awareness of God has nothing to fear in judgment. Such judgment for a person will be to discover what he is and not to condemn or destroy. "Rejoice, O young man, in thy youth; and let thy heart cheer thee in the days of thy youth, and walk in the ways of thine heart, and the sight of thine eyes" (11:9, KJV). The Preacher was not saying that everything young people want to do is sin. A young person who walks with God will go through all of the activities and exuberance of growing up *with God in mind* and will be approved by God when he stands in the judgment. The joy that is so natural to youth, the enthusiasm, the idealism—all of the things of youth that are so positive will be brought into judgment and God will judge how we spent that time.

In the parable of the talents, we see one man who was condemned, but two who were not condemned. Two out of three of them pleased God. We shall all strive to hear him say, "Well done," as he did to these servants. Unaware of judgment, we would allow trivial and vulgar things to control us and we would be lost in a maze of pettiness. For the Christian, the judgment is a time of approval if we stand in his righteousness, power, and purity as we look forward to it.

The Preacher said, in effect, "Know the truth about judgment with such a personal commitment to God that it changes the way you live." We can do that only by his power and grace. In our strength we can never be approved, but God in his mercy has provided righteousness for those who are evil, salvation for those who are lost, approval for those who could never earn it.

We insure his approval by making sure, in the present tense, that we are obedient to the one who will judge— right now, not tomorrow. "Now is the accepted time; behold now is the day of salvation" (2 Cor. 6:2, KJV). "Seek the Lord while he may be found, call ye upon him while he is near" (Isa. 55:6, KJV).

Over and over again the Bible emphasizes that our

response to God must be now. If we are to be approved at judgment, there must be a commitment now. Thus, we live every day of life in the awareness of his presence.

With the Lord in mind, judgment is a reminder of the sweet, precious token of grace that lies ahead. The whole horizon of life is broadened and brightened. No thought, no action, no emotion is insignificant. Everything is seen as the object of him who cares. What a wonderful truth for us!

The conclusion: Reverence God and keep his commandments. This is the whole duty of man. In that way, the judgment can be a time of joy and approval, for the Preacher said, "For God shall bring every work into judgment, with every secret thing, whether it be good, or whether it be evil" (12:14, KJV).